Ultimate Juicing

Delicious Recipes for Over 125 of the Best Fruit and Vegetable Juice Combinations

Donna Pliner Rodnitzky

PRIMA HEALTH

A Division of Prima Publishing

3000 Lava Ridge Court • Roseville, California 95661

(800) 632-8676 • www.primahealth.com

A per serving nutritional breakdown is provided for each recipe. If a range is given for an ingredient amount, the breakdown is based on the smaller number. If a range is given for servings, the breakdown is based on the larger number. If a choice of ingredients is given in an ingredient listing, the breakdown is calculated using the first choice. Nutritional content may vary depending on the specific brands or types of ingredients used. "Optional" ingredients or those for which no specific amount is stated are not included in the breakdown. Nutritional figures are rounded to the nearest whole number.

Warning—disclaimer

This book is not intended to provide medical advice and is sold with the understanding that the publisher and the author are not liable for the misconception or misuse of information provided. The author and Prima Publishing shall have neither liability nor responsibility to any person or entity with respect to any loss, damage, or injury caused or alleged to be caused directly or indirectly by the information contained in this book or the use of any products mentioned.

PRIMA HEALTH and colophon are registered trademarks of Prima Communications, Inc.

Interior illustrations by Sheryl Dickert

Library of Congress Cataloging-in-Publication Data
Rodnitzky, Donna.
   Ultimate juicing: delicious recipes for over 125 of the best fruit and vegetable juice combinations / Donna Pliner Rodnitzky.
   p.   cm.
   Includes index.
   ISBN 0-7615-2576-9
   1. Juicers. 2. Fruit juices. 3. Vegetable juices. I. Title.
TX840.J84 R63   2000
641.8′75—dc21   00-037357
                                                        CIP

00 01 02 03 04 HH 10 9 8 7 6 5 4 3 2 1
Printed in the United States of America

How to Order

Single copies may be ordered from Prima Publishing, 3000 Lava Ridge Court, Roseville, CA 95661; telephone (800) 632-8676, ext. 4444. Quantity discounts are also available. On your letterhead, include information concerning the intended use of the books and the number of books you wish to purchase.

Visit us online at www.primahealth.com

*To my husband, Bob,
to whom I am eternally grateful
for his constant support and guidance
through all my endeavors;
and to my children, David, Adam,
and Laura, whose accomplishments
will always be a source of
tremendous pride for me.*

Contents

Preface

Fresh fruit and vegetable juices have become a favorite healthful indulgence for millions of people. The popularity of juices is reflected by the growing number of juice bars appearing across the nation as well as the expanding variety of juices that are highlighted in the menus of trendy restaurants. But juice is not only to be enjoyed when going out for lunch or dinner. The sheer number and varieties of juicers for sale speaks volumes for the appetite juice lovers have for making their own fresh juice at home and for discovering new and more exciting juice experiences. Today, the availability of juicers in all price ranges means that *every* household can become juice central.

Ultimate Juicing was written for everyone who delights in the great flavor and health benefits derived from drinking fresh juice. Along with 125 recipes for tempting juice combinations, you will also find a comprehensive description of the different kinds of juicers available to help you decide which one will best meet your needs, as well as a discussion of the health benefits derived from juicing. Lastly, you will find an informative discussion of the fruits and vegetables that are best for juicing, along with tips on how to select and process them.

In creating this book, my goal was to develop exciting, fun recipes that would appeal to both the novice juicer and the seasoned juice-meister. For those of you just beginning your adventure in juicing, this book will help you avoid the pitfalls that juice pioneers encountered as they pushed back the frontiers of pulp and rind. For example, even if you adore eating fresh asparagus, don't even think of whipping up a giant glass of asparagus juice. Asparagus is definitely a vegetable that needs other complementary vegetables to be made into a palatable juice. You will learn that by simply adding some carrots and celery, you can create a delicious asparagus juice. The recipes and suggestions you will find here will take you quickly to the head of the juicing class and keep you from having to reinvent the wheel. And for those of you who are experienced juicers, I feel confident that you will be pleased to find many new recipes and ideas that can be added to your existing storehouse of tantalizing recipes.

Now is the time to start squeezing or to expand your juicing horizons. It is my hope that with *Ultimate Juicing* as your guide and inspiration, you will discover the thrill of creating savory vegetable juices, richly sweet fruit juices, or sweet and tangy combinations of both fruit and vegetable juices. So, get your juices flowing, and embark on one of the tastiest and health-filled adventures of your life.

Acknowledgments

I would like to thank Susan Silva, my acquisitions editor, who encouraged and inspired me to write *Ultimate Juicing*, a cookbook that would reflect the high standards of Prima Publishing. I would also like to express my gratitude to my project editor, Michelle McCormack, who has been a pleasure to work with. Thanks to cover designer, Monica Thomas; Sheryl Dickert, illustrator; and the entire staff at Prima Publishing for their excellent professionalism in bringing this book to publication.

Introduction

Many of us have fond memories of our family seated around a kitchen table laden with an array of delicious homemade breakfast items. Of course, before we could start eating, the first order of business was to drink a tall glass of freshly squeezed orange juice. Unfortunately, with the passage of time, canned orange juice concentrate or cartons of pasteurized juice have gradually replaced the freshly squeezed variety, and microwaved muffins come to be the only warm item on the breakfast plate. Although for many of us the family breakfast may be a relic of the past, millions of people are rediscovering the great taste and health benefits of freshly squeezed orange juice, as well as the limitless number of other fresh fruit and vegetable juices.

Today, juices aren't only for breakfast. Friends and business acquaintances look forward to meeting for a glass of healthful cheer at their favorite juice bar or at a restaurant. But the most impressive increasing trend is the number of us preparing fresh juice at home. Those of us who own juicers have discovered that freshly prepared juice is a treat at home for family and friends at any time of the day, not just before hurrying off to school or work in the morning.

Whether your lifestyle is busy or serene, juices allow you to reap the benefits of fresh fruits and vegetables in your diet with very little effort.

I wrote this book to appeal to you and the millions of other people who have discovered, or who are just beginning to discover, the wonderful flavor and health benefits derived from drinking fresh juice. Most important, it was written to make juicing more fun and an exciting experience for both the novice and the veteran juicer. *Ultimate Juicing* begins by providing you with all the information you will need to make your juicing experience most satisfying. You will find an informative analysis of the different kinds of juicers on the market to help you decide which one would be best for you. I've also provided detailed information on how to select, prepare, and store the choicest fruits and vegetables for juicing. Another chapter discusses the health benefits of juicing.

The rest of the book stars over 125 tempting recipes that I hope you will not only enjoy but will also use as an inspiration to create your own taste treats. Whether you are a first-time juicer or an expert, you will be delighted with chapter 4, "Back to Basics: Classic Juice Combinations." It includes a multitude of fruit and vegetable combinations that will introduce you to the artistry of blending juices. Once you have experienced the ease of making these juices and the delicious results, you will be on your way to creating your own masterpieces.

Chapter 5, "Power Juices for Your Health" is devoted to juices that are designed to be still healthier than most. How can that be possible when fresh juices are already so naturally healthful? In these recipes, you will see how easy it is to add health-enhancing supplements to juice without appreciably changing its taste or consistency. For example, Ginseng in the Rain is a delightful combination of raspberries, apple, cantaloupe, and health-promoting ginseng. You will also find a detailed discussion of the role of wheatgrass in juicing, followed by several enticing recipes. I must admit that I was very skeptical of how wheatgrass juice would taste and concerned that I might not react well to it. To my pleasant surprise, I found the taste appealing and the effect (an energy boost) exhilarating. In fact, one of my favorite recipes is Wheatgrass Hopper, a simple combination of pineapple juice and wheatgrass. This delightful combination has now become a regular treat for me.

Chapter 6, "Excitement in a Glass: Exotic Juices in Your Own Kitchen," will introduce to you juices that are a bit out of the ordinary. You will discover how exciting it can be to add a zesty condiment or spice to your own creation or to incorporate an unusual fruit or vegetable. So, treat yourself to a glass of The Beet Goes On, made with beet, carrot, yam, garlic, and ginger, or for a sweet indulgence, try First Mango on the Moon, made with mango, pineapple, and lime. Once you have enjoyed these exotic delights, experiment a bit by adding or substituting one more interesting ingredient. What you will soon begin to realize is that you have hidden creative talents you never knew existed.

Chapter 7, "Shaken but Not Stirred: Juicing Cocktails" was great fun in the making.

Many alcoholic drinks include a healthful dose of fresh juice. Most often, the canned or bottled variety is used for the ease of it and to save time. However, once you have tasted a rum drink, such as a Mai Tai, made with fresh pineapple juice, you will be spoiled forever. Serve the drink in a cocktail glass garnished with a fresh orchid, then relax and wait for the rave reviews.

Speaking of garnishes, you will be delighted with the last chapter, "Garnishes with a Twist," which focuses on those little details that can make a glass of juice special. Of course, there is no denying that the most important ingredient is the juice. However, for those few occasions when a special drink is in order, this chapter will provide you with a host of garnishes with real eye appeal, ranging from a simple slice of orange to a more exotic Lemon and Cranberry Twist. These garnishes can add a dash of color, flavor, or interest to any drink, even a simple glass of orange juice.

Whether you prefer fruit or vegetable juice, or a combination of both, this book is for you. So discard those cartons and bottles taking up valuable space in your refrigerator and join the ranks of the millions of people who have discovered the satisfaction and benefits of preparing fresh juice.

Health Benefits of Juicing

*W*ith today's trend toward a more healthy lifestyle, it should come as no surprise that fresh fruit and vegetable juices have been steadily gaining in popularity. Like the ascent of eating salads in the 1980s, drinking fresh juice became the new boom for the 1990s and into the new millennium. Millions of us have discovered that drinking fruit and vegetable juices is a natural way to fulfill our bodies' needs for critical nutrients, and if that weren't a great enough enticement, fresh juices are also delicious and virtually fat-free and low in calories, cholesterol, and sodium.

Health authorities, such as the National Cancer Institute, send a recurring message that we must include more fruits and vegetables in our daily diets to reduce the risk of a variety of serious ailments. But accommodating the recommended three to five servings of vegetables and two to three servings of fruit each day in an ordinary diet can be difficult. The good news is that even with a hectic lifestyle, we can still achieve this lofty goal by simply including fresh juices as part of our daily diets. Can you think of a better, or easier, way to accomplish this than by enjoying a tall glass of fresh carrot juice made with eight carrots or a chilled glass of apple juice made with three to four apples? By just adding two to three glasses of juice to your diet, you can quickly satisfy your daily requirements and at the same time enjoy a great taste experience. Juicing fruits and vegetables essentially eliminates their indigestible insoluble fiber and enhances the availability of important nutrients. For example, when you eat a fresh carrot, many of the important nutrients become trapped in the fiber so that you only assimilate approximately 1 percent of the vegetable's available beta-carotene. But when you juice a carrot and remove the fiber, almost 100 percent of the beta-carotene is absorbable. By drinking the fresh juice of many other fruits and vegetables, you are able to more easily digest and absorb the maximum number of nutrients and enzymes they provide within minutes.

On the subject of enzymes, they are the body's workforce. They spark thousands of chemical reactions that occur throughout our bodies and are responsible for most of our metabolic activity every second of the day. Enzymes play an essential role in digesting and absorbing food, converting food into body tissue, and in producing energy at the cellular level. This is one more reason that drinking fresh fruit and vegetable juices is especially important in maintaining good health.

Another advantage of drinking fresh fruit and vegetable juices is the health benefit of true freshness. None of the vital nutrients are lost when juice is consumed *immediately* after it is made. Just as important, no additives, preservatives, sugars, or sweeteners are added, and the juice has not been pasteurized to extend its shelf life. Fresh juice is absolutely pure, and you know exactly what it contains.

As scientists have learned more about the bounty of antioxidants found in fresh fruits and vegetables, it has become increasingly apparent why it is important to enrich our diets with these nutrient-packed powerhouses. Today, this goal can be easily achieved with a few flavorful swallows, since drinking three 8-ounce glasses of juice can provide the nutritional benefits of up to 3 pounds of fresh fruits or vegetables.

The list of health benefits goes on and on. For example, it is extremely important to include a healthy amount of liquid in our diets. When you drink fruit or vegetable juices, you are also consuming untreated pure water. More than 65 percent of the tissues and cells in our bodies is water. Water also acts as a conduit for carrying necessary nutrients and blood cells through our bodies. By drinking an adequate amount of water, we put less stress on our bodies and promote the smooth operation of their natural processes.

As you glance through chapter 5 "Power Juices for Your Health," you will become aware of a number of recipes that include health boosters to enhance juices that are already inherently healthful. These ingredients can be eliminated if you like your juice straight; however, I have included them for those who prefer an added health benefit to their diet regimens. Examples of some of the health boosters you will find are:

- **Bee pollen**
  This natural substance is thought to increase sexual performance and stamina. It is 35 percent protein and contains twenty-seven minerals, most of the known vitamins, as well as many enzymes.

- **Echinacea**
  This herb boosts the immune system and is especially helpful when you are ailing from a cold.

- **Gingko Biloba**
  This extract comes from the fan-shaped leaf of the gingko tree. It is thought to increase blood flow to the brain and enhance several of its functions, such as memory.

- **Ginseng**
  Another herb believed to be capable of normalizing various body functions, increasing mental alertness and vitality, relieving stress, and enhancing immunity.

- **Vitamin C**
  This critical nutrient buttresses the immune system to help increase resistance to cancer.

So, the next time you want to treat yourself to a wholesome taste sensation, head for the nearest juice bar and hope a seat is available. Better yet, don't take the chance that there may be standing room only and invest in a juicer so that your health takes center stage in your own home.

CHAPTER 2

The Perfect Produce

How to Select, Prepare, and Store Fresh Fruits and Vegetables

*A*fter extensive research, comparison shopping, checking out the Internet, and polling friends, you are ready to make a wise decision and purchase a juicer that is perfect for your needs and pocketbook. There is nothing more important than learning as much as possible about the wide variety of fruits and vegetables available for juicing is equally important. For example, it can be very helpful to know that broccoli or kale juice on its own may be too strong or unpalatable for most people's taste. On the other hand, realizing that carrot juice is inherently sweet may prompt you to combine it with many of the strong-flavored vegetables, resulting in a zesty combination. The same can be said for some fruits. Lemon and lime juice alone would be less than a sweet reward; however, when either is blended with pineapple or mango, the juice magically transports you to a tropical paradise.

In this chapter, I will provide you with all the information you will need to select the best fruits and vegetables for creating a delectable juice. I will also suggest which can stand alone and which are best combined. Lastly, as I have tried to stress throughout this book, preparing fresh juice is an individual experience that can be a creative trip. My hope is that as you become more familiar with the fabulous array of produce available, the excitement of making fresh juices will inspire you to create your own recipes.

VEGETABLES

Vegetables have graduated from their traditional side dish and salad roles to become a star ingredient, reaching new creative heights when combined with other produce in fresh juices. Here's a rundown on some of the best and most healthful veggies around.

Asparagus

Asparagus is native to the Mediterranean area of southern Europe and is said to have been cultivated for more than two thousand years. In 1700, Dutch and English colonists brought asparagus to America, where it was first planted in New England.

The asparagus is a member of the lily family. The young shoot is the edible part and can range in color from green or white to purple. It is usually available from mid-February through

July, with the peak season being from April through June. It is an excellent source of vitamin A.

When buying asparagus, look for stalks that are straight with closed, compact buds. In the spring, choose spears that are pencil-thin. As the season progresses, the fatter ones will taste best. Also, look at the stem end to confirm that it has been freshly cut and is not dried out, because asparagus begins to lose its sweetness soon after it is cut. Wash the asparagus and store in the coldest part of the refrigerator, with the base of the spears wrapped in a damp paper towel. Although it is best to eat asparagus the day it is purchased, it will keep in the refrigerator for four or five days.

Asparagus juice is best when combined with the juice of other vegetables, such as carrots. Cut the asparagus in sizes just large enough to fit in your juicer.

Beets

The beet is native to the Mediterranean region. When the Romans first began to eat beets, they consumed only the leafy part. It was not until the Christian era that they began to eat the root part of the beet. Beets are a good source of iron and calcium, while the greens are rich in iron, calcium, and vitamin A.

When choosing beets, look for those that are small to medium in size with smooth, unblemished skins and fresh, crisp leaves. Wash them well, and if they must be stored, place them in an airtight plastic bag in the refrigerator where they should keep for up to three weeks.

Beet juice should not be consumed alone because it can cause irritation to the throat and esophagus. Instead, combine the beet and beet top with any of the milder fruits and vegetables such as carrots, apples, or celery.

Broccoli

Up until the 1920s in the United States, broccoli was mostly known to and consumed by Italian immigrants. Once others outside this community learned of its versatility and extensive nutritional content, it rapidly gained in popularity. Today, broccoli is recognized as being an excellent source of calcium as well as being exceptionally high in the important antioxidants, vitamins C and E, and a host of other cancer-fighting phyto-chemicals. Broccoli, a member of the cruciferous family, can be eaten raw, cooked, or juiced.

When choosing broccoli, look for ones that have tightly closed green clusters, firm stalks, and a fresh aroma, rather than a cabbage smell. Avoid any with yellow florets, dried ends, or a woody stem. Wash broccoli well, and when dry, store it in an airtight plastic bag in the re-frigerator.

Broccoli juice has a strong flavor if you drink it alone. Before juicing broccoli, separate it into florets with stems just large enough to fit in your juicer. Three to four broccoli florets can be added to many of the vegetable recipes found in the "Back to Basics" chapter for a delicious and nutrient-filled juice.

Brussels Sprouts

Brussels sprouts are a member of the cruciferous family and are therefore related to cabbage and cauliflower. When first sprouting, the vegetable's stem sends up a long shoot with the sprouts forming close to the ground. As the sprouts, others appear higher up on the stalk. Each one looks like a small head of cabbage, measuring from ½ to 1 inch in diameter. Not surprisingly, brussels sprouts were first cultivated in Brussels. They are an excellent source of vitamins A and C and are in season from September through January.

When choosing brussels sprouts, look for ones that are green and firm. Select those with smaller heads for their more delicate flavor. Avoid any with yellow or wilted leaves. Store the brussels sprouts in an airtight plastic bag in the refrigerator and wash them just before they are ready to be used.

Brussels sprout juice has a strong flavor used alone. Before juicing them, separate the brussels sprouts into individual heads with stems just large enough to fit in your juicer. Consider adding three to four brussels sprouts to some of the vegetable recipes found in the "Back to Basics" chapter, such as Carrot and Apple or Carrot and Cucumber.

Cabbage

Cabbage is considered to be the most ancient cultivated leafy plant. It is native to England and northwest France but is now widely grown throughout Europe, Asia, and America. A member of the cruciferous family, it is related to other vegetables such as brussels sprouts, broccoli, kale, and cauliflower, to name a few. There are three kinds of cabbage, each with leaves that grow close together to form a round head. The leaves of the Savoy variety are wrinkled, while those of the white cabbage are pale and smooth with raised veins. Red cabbage has leaves similar to the white variety except for their purplish-red color. Cabbage is an excellent source of vitamin C.

When choosing a head of cabbage, look for one that is firm, heavy for its size, and has closely trimmed stems. Avoid any cabbage that has discoloration of the leaves. Wash the cabbage well and store in the refrigerator.

Cabbage juice alone is very strong and should be combined with the juice of other vegetables, such as carrots. Before juicing, cut the cabbage into wedges just large enough to fit in your juicer.

Carrots

The carrot is a long, orange root vegetable native to Afghanistan. It is known to have been cultivated in the Mediterranean area as long ago as 500 B.C. Originally, this vegetable was used for medicinal purposes rather than a food source. By the sixteenth century in Europe, improved methods of cultivating the carrot allowed it quickly to gain in popularity as an excellent food. Carrots are a very good source of vitamins A, B, C, beta-carotene and other carotenoids. Darker carrots contain more carotene, a substance the body converts into vitamin A.

When choosing carrots, buy those that are firm and void of any cracks. Carrots with new green sprouts or a wide diameter may have a woody core. In general, a brighter color usually means a sweeter carrot. Carrots should be washed well. If nonorganic carrots are used, remove the tip and core end because pesticides are more concentrated there. Refrigerate this vegetable until ready to use.

Carrot juice alone is delicious, but because it is mild-flavored, it combines well with the juice of most vegetables, especially those in the cruciferous family, such as broccoli, kale, cabbage, and cauliflower. It also blends nicely with some fruits, such as pineapple, apple, and pear. Cut unpeeled carrots into 2- to 3-inch lengths just large enough to fit in your juicer.

Cauliflower

Cauliflower originated in Asia, but the present-day cauliflower that we know was perfected in Italy. It is a member of the cruciferous family. It has a large head made up of edible, creamy white, clustered, juicy flowers that are surrounded by large green leaves. It is very high in vitamin C.

When choosing cauliflower, look for heads that are creamy white and void of any spots that indicate it may not be fresh. Wash the cauliflower well, and when dry, store in the refrigerator.

Cauliflower juice alone is very strong and should be combined with the juice of other vegetables and fruits, such as carrots or apples. Before juicing a cauliflower, break it into florets with stems just large enough to fit in your juicer.

Try adding two to four florets to some of the recipes in the "Back to Basics" chapter.

Celery

Celery has been enjoyed as a food source for almost three thousand years, although its exact origin is unknown. It is native to the Mediterranean region of Europe. The variety most often found in the United States is the Pascal type, which is green with upright crisp, large, succulent leaf stalks. This variety is less stringy and has a pronounced flavor. Celery is high in vitamin C and potassium.

When choosing celery, look for those with firm stalks and fresh-looking leaves. Also, the rib of the head should break with a clean snap when bent. Whether you buy organic or non-organic celery, cut the end off and separate the stalks. Wash the celery well, wrap it in paper towels, and store in a very dark, cool place or the refrigerator.

To juice celery, cut it into 2- to 3-inch lengths and add them to the juicer along with the leaves.

Cucumbers

Cucumbers are known to be one of the oldest cultivated crops, dating back to ancient Babylon. They are native to Thailand and have been cultivated in western Asia for three thousand years. After cucumbers spread to Europe, the Spaniards brought them to Haiti in 1494, and by the late 1500s, they were being cultivated in the

Americas. Cucumbers are an excellent source of vitamins C and A, potassium, and folate.

When choosing a cucumber, look for one that is firm and has a dark green skin with small lumps. Avoid any that are soft or have a wrinkled skin. Wash the cucumbers well and refrigerate.

To juice the cucumber, peel away the waxed skin and cut the cucumber into cubes or spears. Cucumber juice should be combined with the juice of other fruits and vegetables. Many of the recipes in the "Back to Basics" chapter would be an excellent choice for this melding of tastes.

Fennel

Florence (or bulb) fennel dates back to ancient Rome, where it was eaten as a digestive aid, palate cleanser, and breath freshener. It has a large white bulb with heavy stalks that resemble celery and soft feathery leaves that look like dill. The bulb of the fennel is used to make a juice.

Although fennel is available year-round, it is a winter vegetable, its main season being October through April. When selecting a fennel, choose one with a heavy, firm bulb that is about the size of a tennis ball and is white with no bruising. Rounder bulbs tend to be sweeter, and their licorice flavor is less pronounced than the flattened variety. The feathery leaves should be bright green with stalks that are firm, which indicates its freshness. Avoid any cut fennel because it will not be as flavorful.

Fennel should be used within a few days after purchase. Remove the stalks and leaves with a knife and wash them well. Wrap the bulb in plastic wrap and refrigerate.

Before juicing, cut the fennel in half or in wedges just large enough to fit in your juicer. Because it has a distinctive anise flavor, fennel juice tastes best when mixed with the juice of other mild-flavored fruits and vegetables, such as cucumbers, apples, or pears.

Garlic

Garlic is highly valued for its impressive health benefits. The most important is its ability to increase HDL ("good") cholesterol levels, which play a major role in protecting against heart disease and may also lower blood pressure in some individuals. However, garlic has not always been so highly esteemed. It is a native of Asia, but once garlic arrived in Europe, it received mixed reviews. Ancient Greeks disliked it, so they forbade recent garlic eaters to enter into the Temple of Cybele. The Romans, on the other hand, were divided about their attitudes toward garlic, with the nobles disapproving of it but otherwise recommending it as a healthful food for the masses.

Garlic is a bulbous member of the lily family. The heads may be covered with a papery white, pink, or mauve skin. Each head is divided into ten to twelve sections, or cloves. When choosing garlic, select cloves that are plump and firm and avoid any that are shriveled or dried out. Store in a cool, dark place in a well-ventilated bag or basket.

Add one to two cloves to the juicer, followed by the vegetables of your choice. This will help rid most of the typical garlic aroma from the juicer. Garlic can also be enclosed in a leafy vegetable or green before being added to the juicer.

Ginger

Ginger comes from the rootstock of a reedy, herbaceous plant, *Zingiber officinale*. It is thought to be native to India, as well as other countries in tropical Asia. It was the first spice to be transplanted to the New World. Today, the finest ginger comes from India and Jamaica. The whole ginger is light brown and knotty on the outside and golden and juicy on the inside. It has an exotic sweet-and-spicy flavor.

When choosing ginger, look for ones that are firm and void of any soft spots or wrinkled skin. Store the ginger in a cool, dark place in a well-ventilated bag or basket.

Before juicing ginger, remove the skin. Depending on how hot and spicy you like your juice, you might want to start with a scant ¼-inch slice. If the result is not hot enough, gradually increase the amount to what appeals to your palate.

Jicama

The jicama (pronounced hik'-a-ma) is a leguminous plant with a very large tuberous root. There are two types. The yam bean, the smaller of the two, is found in the tropics of both hemispheres. The larger variety is cultivated in the temperate and tropical regions of America and considered to be a major crop of Mexico. Jicama has a thin, light brown skin. The inside is crisp and has a flavor similar to apples and water chestnuts. Jicamas are a good source of potassium, calcium, and phosphorous.

When choosing a jicama, look for one that is firm and heavy for its size. Avoid any that are shriveled or larger than average. Wash the jicama, and when dry, store it in a dark, cool place.

To juice a jicama, remove the skin and cut into wedges or cubes large enough to fit in your juicer. Jicama juice is best combined with the juice of other vegetables.

Kale

Kale is a winter vegetable that is very similar to cabbage except that its leaves are loose and curly, rather than shaped like a head. It is native to Europe, where it was cultivated for centuries to feed both people and animals. It is an excellent source of vitamins A, B, and C.

When choosing kale, look for one that has crisp, dark green leaves. Avoid any with thick or yellow leaves. Use the same method for washing and drying the kale as is suggested in the lettuce section. Wrap the leaves in paper towels and store in the refrigerator.

To juice kale, the leaves can be added whole or broken into appropriate sizes, depending on the size of your juicer. Kale juice is best when combined with the juice of other mild-flavored vegetables, such as carrots.

Lettuce

The cultivation of lettuce began in Persia as long ago as 500 B.C. Because lettuce is sweet and juicy, it is a perfect salad green to add to a juice. In addition, it is an excellent source of vitamins A, B, C, and E, as well as calcium, iron, and magnesium.

When selecting lettuce, always choose those with fresh, crisp leaves and a garden-fresh smell. Avoid any that are spotted with brown marks or have oversized or wilted leaves.

Many greens are now available prewashed and packaged in airtight bags. However, I still recommend washing them. If you do not have a salad spinner, the greens will have to be washed and dried by hand. A simple way to do this is to tear the leaves into large pieces and immerse them in a pot or sink filled with cold water. Swish the leaves around with your hands to remove any grit. They can also be rinsed under cold running water. Once the leaves are washed, the next step is to dry them. As you scoop up the leaves with your hands, look for any that are brown and wilted and remove them. Then gently shake the leaves to remove as much water as possible. After the greens are dry, place them in a salad crisper or wrap them loosely in a paper or cloth towel. Roll up the towel and place it in a refrigerator bag, poking holes in the bag to allow any moisture to escape. Refrigerate the greens until ready to use.

To insert lettuce into a juicer, first take a small portion of leaves and mold them into a ball, then push it through the feed tube. Lettuce juice is best when combined with the juice of other vegetables, such as carrots and celery.

Because of the wide variety of lettuce available, you should be aware of the leafier ones that are best for juicing. These are a few of my favorites, but please don't hesitate to experiment with some of yours.

Butterhead Lettuce

These greens are sometimes referred to as "hearting lettuce" because the inner leaves are packed tightly together, while farther from the center, the leaves are larger and softer. All the leaves can be added to a juice, but the inner leaves, or heart, are the most tender and sweet. The two varieties of butterhead are Boston (butter) lettuce and Bibb (Kentucky limestone) lettuce. When choosing butterhead lettuce, look for a head that is crisp and has a white base with bright green leaves on the outer edge.

Loose-Leaf Lettuce

This variety of lettuce includes red leaf and oak leaf. It has large, frilly, and curly leaves that are most often light green but can also be shaded with red. Because the leaves are somewhat thinner than those of other varieties, it is best to use them as soon as possible.

Romaine (Cos) Lettuce

This lettuce is named for the Greek island of Cos where it originated. It has long, coarse green outer leaves, but the white leaves in the center are the tastiest and crispiest.

Parsley

Parsley, a member of the carrot family, is native to the Mediterranean region and believed to have first been cultivated in Sardinia and Italy.

There are four types: Neapolitan parsley, grown for its stalks and similar to celery; Hamburg parsley, grown for its roots; curly parsley; and flat-leaf parsley. The latter two are the varieties most often available in produce departments. Parsley is rich in vitamins A and C as well as iron and calcium.

When choosing parsley, look for a bunch with crisp, dark green leaves. Avoid any with yellow leaves. Wash thoroughly and when dry, wrap the parsley in paper towels and store in an airtight plastic bag in the refrigerator.

To juice parsley, add seven to eight sprigs to the juicer. Parsley juice is best when combined with the juice of other vegetables, especially carrots.

Pepper (Bell)

Bell peppers are native to Mexico and Central and South America. In the fifteenth century, Spanish explorers discovered sweet and hot peppers in the West Indies and took samples back to Europe where they quickly became popular as a food, condiment, and spice pepper. A few decades later, bell peppers were found growing throughout the West Indies and the Americas. The common varieties of bell peppers ripen on the vine, and the riper the bell pepper, the sweeter it is. Bell peppers—whether green, yellow, or red—are a good source of vitamin C.

When choosing a bell pepper, look for a firm one that has a glossy skin with a sheen rather than one with a wrinkled appearance. Wash the bell pepper and store it in the refrigerator.

To juice a bell pepper, cut the pepper into cubes or quarters, just large enough to fit in the juicer. Because a bell pepper has a very strong, distinct flavor, it is best when combined in small quantities with the juice of other vegetables, such as carrots.

Spinach

Spinach is believed to have originated in Persia or Southwest Asia and was cultivated by the Greeks and Romans long before the Christian era. The leaves of spinach are high in vitamins A, B, C, E, and K, as well as iron, phosphorous, and fiber.

When choosing spinach, look for leaves that are dark green, firm, and crisp with short stems. It should also have a fresh fragrance. Because spinach is a low-growing plant, it should be washed well to remove any sand or grit. Even pre-washed spinach that comes prepackaged should be washed before use. You can use the same method for washing, drying, and storing the spinach as suggested in the lettuce section.

To insert spinach into a juicer, first take a small portion of the leaves and mold them into a ball, then push the ball through the feed tube. Spinach juice is best when combined with the juice of other vegetables, such as carrots or celery.

String Beans

String beans, sometimes called snap beans, are the whole, immature pods of different types of kidney beans. Kidney beans were first cultivated by the Indians of Central and South America. They are an excellent source of vitamins A, B, and C.

When choosing string beans, look for those that are plump, heavy, and break with a clean snap when bent. Wash the beans well, and when dry, place them in an airtight plastic bag in the refrigerator for a few days.

Before juicing, cut the string beans in appropriate lengths large enough to fit in your juicer. Because string bean juice alone has a strong flavor, it is best when combined with the juice of other vegetables, such as carrots or celery.

Tomatoes

The tomato is a fruit native to Peru, but is often called a vegetable because of the way it is eaten and served. It was first cultivated as early as 700 A.D. by the Aztecs and Incas. In the 1500s, tomato seeds were introduced to Europe when the Conquistadors returned from Mexico and Central America, but people were afraid to eat the fruit because it belonged to the poisonous nightshade family. It was not until the 1800s that tomatoes became widely used.

Ripe tomatoes are most often red, although they come in a variety of colors when mature ranging from green and yellow to orange. At the same time, size and shape also vary widely: Some tomatoes are as small as cherries, while others, such as the beefsteak tomato, are as large as a grapefruit. The shapes can also range from being perfectly round to pear-shaped, lobed, or oblong.

The hundreds of varieties of tomatoes can easily be sorted into four categories. Beefsteak tomatoes are very large and juicy and are either lobed or globe-like in shape. Cherry tomatoes are small and up to an inch in diameter. Sauce tomatoes are made up of the oval, oblong, or long variety. Finally, the slicers are great for anything, including juicing. Most are globe-shaped. All tomatoes are an excellent source of vitamins A and C and potassium.

When choosing a tomato, look for one that has a shiny skin, is heavy for its size, has a nice aroma, and has a slight give to it. If the stem calyx is still attached, it should be green and fresh-looking. If organic tomatoes are available, they are the best choice. Wash the tomatoes and refrigerate them to retain their flavor.

To juice a tomato, cut it into appropriate-size wedges that will fit in your juicer. Tomato juice is delicious on its own but also combines well with the juice of other vegetables, such as carrots, parsley, and celery.

Yams and Sweet Potatoes

Yams and sweet potatoes are frequently confused because they are very similar in size, texture, flavor, and shape. Although they are both tubers, they belong to different botanical families. The sweet potato, an edible root of the *Ipomoea batatas* species of plants, originated in the Western Hemisphere and has either a dark red skin with a moist, deep orange flesh or a tan skin with a dry, yellow flesh. The true yam, a member of the *Dioscorea* genus, originated in Asia and Africa, and it is believed that African slaves introduced them to the New World. Yams have a rough brown skin with yellow, white, or purple flesh. Yams and sweet potatoes are both very high in vitamins C and A, as well as potassium and fiber.

When choosing sweet potatoes and yams, look for ones that are firm and fresh-looking. Wash and store them in a dark, cool place.

To juice a sweet potato or yam, cut either one into cubes or wedges just large enough to fit into your juicer. Sweet potato or yam juice is best when combined with the juice of other vegetables, such as carrots and beets.

Wheatgrass

The plant wheatgrass is grown from the red wheatberry. This special strain of grass yields high concentrations of chlorophyll, vitamins, active enzymes, and other nutrients. Seventy percent of the solid content of wheatgrass is chlorophyll, which is the basis of all plant life and very closely resembles the molecular structure of hemoglobin, the oxygen-carrying protein of human red blood cells. Wheatgrass juice contains an abundance of enzymes not found in cooked or processed foods. Wheatgrass is also rich in vitamins A, complete B complex, B_{17}, C, E, and K. It is a superb source of calcium, potassium, iron, magnesium, phosphorous, sodium, sulfur, cobalt, and zinc, as well as every known essential amino acid (those the human body cannot manufacture itself).

Based on its rich content of vitamins, minerals, enzymes, antioxidants, and amino acids, many deem wheatgrass to be "nature's finest medicine." Some of the health roles that have been attributed to wheatgrass are that it:

- Stimulates metabolism

- Helps fight anemia

- Neutralizes carcinogens and toxins in the body

- Improves digestion

- Aids in the protection of your body from the harmful effects of free radicals and radiation

- Lowers your cholesterol level and reduces the risks of heart disease

- Deters unfriendly bacterial growth

- Provides energy

- Aids in the prevention of some cancers

The suggested amount of wheatgrass juice for first-time users is 1 ounce a day, since some individuals feel nauseous if they ingest too much. Once you feel comfortable with that amount, you can gradually increase the amount to 1 to 2 ounces three times a day.

To make wheatgrass juice, you need a special wheatgrass juicer. Information on this kind of juicer can be found in chapter 3, "Selecting a Juicer."

Wheatgrass is available at most health food stores. The Internet is also a good source for finding it; companies such as Wheatgrass Express will ship fresh wheatgrass via Federal Express overnight.

Wheatgrass should always be washed and dried before using. To make wheatgrass juice, first take a small portion of it and compress it into a ball, then insert it into the feed tube of the juicer. This makes the process easier and neater. A shot of wheatgrass is delicious on its own, but you may prefer to combine it with the juice of other fruits and vegetables, such as pineapple, apples, and carrots.

FRUIT

Why settle for the ordinary o.j. when so many other fruit juices, alone and in combination, make for a zesty refreshment any time of day? Here's a sampling of the bounty awaiting you in the fruit department of your favorite grocery.

Apples

Apples are believed to have originated in Central Asia and Caucasus, but they have been cultivated since prehistoric times. They were brought to the United States at the beginning of the seventeenth century and later to Africa and Australia. Today, over a hundred varieties of apples are commercially grown in the United States.

The apple is a small, round fruit that can be red, green, or yellow, with a firm, crisp flesh. Some apples have a sweet flavor with a hint of tartness, while others are less sweet and more tart. Unpeeled apples are high in fiber. All apples are delicious when made into a juice, but your flavor preference will determine which one is best for you.

When choosing an apple, look for one that is firm and crisp with a smooth, tight skin. Most important, the apple should have a sweet-smelling aroma. Avoid any apple that has bruised or blemished skin. Another consideration when choosing apples is to buy those grown organically, whenever possible. Most nonorganic apples are heavily sprayed with pesticides and later waxed to preserve them to be kept looking fresh, while the organically grown variety are not. Because of this, you might encounter a worm in some organic apples, which can be removed when the apple is cut, thereby removing any health or aesthetic concerns. Wash apples well, whether organic or not, and refrigerate.

To juice an apple with a waxed skin, remove the skin first. All apples should be cut into eighths or wedges, depending on the size of your juicer.

Because of the vast number of apple varieties, I have included several of the more popular ones that I feel are an excellent choice for juicing.

Fuji

These apples are newcomers to the apple arena but have become immensely popular because they are very sweet in flavor and juicy. These apples are available October through December.

Golden Delicious

The Golden Delicious apple has a pale green to yellow skin. Those with yellow skins are sweeter and most delicious. Although harvested in

October, these apples are available year-round. Because of this timetable, Golden Delicious apples should generally be avoided in the spring and summer, when they tend to be soft.

Granny Smith

Granny Smith apples are more tart than most other varieties. Those with a paler green skin are usually riper, sweeter, and more mature. These apples are harvested in October and are available year-round.

Jonagold

These sweet and juicy apples are harvested in late September and are at their best when just picked.

McIntosh

McIntosh apples are very sweet in flavor. They do not keep as well as other apples so they are best eaten or juiced soon after they are harvested in September.

Red Delicious

This apple lives up to its name. It is deep purplish red and has a distinctive, five-knob base. It is considered to be the world's leading variety of apple. Its harvesting time is similar to the Golden Delicious.

Apricots

The apricot is a round or oblong fruit, measuring about 2 inches in diameter, whose skin and flesh are orange-yellow. It is very sweet and juicy and has a single, smooth stone. The apricot is native to northern China and was known to be a food source as early as 2200 B.C. Apricots are an excellent source of vitamin A, potassium, and iron.

When choosing apricots, look for those that are well colored and firm but yield slightly when gently pressed. Avoid any that are green or yellow because this may indicate they are not ripe, while soft ones are probably overripe. Wash apricots and keep them refrigerated until ready to use.

To juice an apricot, remove the stone and cut the apricot in half before adding to the juicer.

Asian Pears

The fruit of a tree that originated in Asia, the Asian pear is believed to be the ancestor of all the pears we eat today. It has a distinct pear-like taste but is crisp in texture like an apple. Many also have a round shape resembling an apple. Because of this similarity in taste, appearance, and shape, Asian pears are often called "apple-pears."

Asian pears are round with a pale, yellow or golden-brown skin. Whether eaten raw or juiced, the skin should always be removed. Wash the pears and store them in the refrigerator for up to two months.

To juice an Asian pear, peel the skin and cut into wedges just large enough to fit into a juicer. Asian pear juice is especially delicious when combined with the juice of other fruits.

Bananas

The banana is not a good fruit to add to a juicer because it is too soft, but when combined with other fresh fruit juices in a blender, you can add a sensational banana flavor to your juice. If you blend a frozen banana with chilled fruit juice and some ice, you can create a luscious smoothie.

The banana has been around for so long that, according to Hindu legend, it was actually the forbidden fruit of the Garden of Eden. It is also believed that the banana was widely cultivated throughout Asia and Oceania before recorded history and that the Spanish colonists introduced banana shoots to the New World in 1516. Bananas are a rich source of vitamins A, B, C, and B_2, as well as potassium.

When choosing a banana, look for one that is completely yellow. Green bananas will ripen at room temperature in two days. Once ripe, they can be stored in the refrigerator for a couple of days.

Blueberries

Native to North America, the blueberry is the second most popular berry in the United States. It has been around for thousands of years but wasn't cultivated until the turn of the century. Today, 95 percent of the world's commercial blueberry crops are grown in the United States. Blueberries are at their peak in flavor from mid-April to late September. They are available in the southern states first and gradually move north as the season progresses. Blueberries are an excellent source of vitamin C and fiber.

When choosing blueberries, look for ones that are deep-purple blue to blue-black, dry, smooth-skinned, plump, and firm. Avoid any that appear to be dull or soft and watery because this may indicate that the fruit is old. Store the blueberries in the refrigerator for up to 10 days and wash them just before using.

Blueberry juice is especially delicious when combined with other fruit juices, such as pineapple, apples, or pears.

Cherries

Cherries are small, round, red to black fruit that grow on a tree. There are numerous varieties, but all of them fall into one of three categories: sweet, sour, or a hybrid of the two. Cherries grow in the temperate zones of Europe, Asia, and the Americas. It is believed that they originated in northeastern Asia and later spread throughout the temperate zones in prehistory, carried by birds who ate the cherries and later dropped the stones. Sweet cherries make the most flavorful juice. They are a source of vitamin C and fiber.

When choosing cherries, look for those that are dark, plump, and firm. Store the cherries in the refrigerator and wash them just before using.

To juice a cherry, remove the stone before adding it to the juicer. Cherry juice is delicious on its own but will also combine nicely with most fruit juices.

Citrus Fruits: Grapefruit, Lemon, Lime, Orange, and Tangerine

Citrus fruits growing in Southeast Asia have been recorded by Chinese agriculturists some eight hundred years ago. During the expansion of the Roman Empire, citrus was cultivated in Italy. Later it spread with the Arab Empire into North Africa, Spain, and the lands surrounding the Mediterranean Sea. In 1493, Christopher Columbus brought many varieties of citrus to Haiti on his second voyage to the New World; by 1525, they were widespread and abundant. In the early part of the sixteenth century, Spanish explorers brought citrus with them to trade with the Indians. Citrus trees soon began to grow wild in Florida near rivers and lakes from seeds that were dropped by the Indians.

Grapefruits

The first seedless grapefruit (nine seeds or less) was discovered in Florida in the 1800s, while the first pink seedless grapefruit was also found in Florida in 1913. In the early 1920s, seedless grapefruit began to be cultivated in the richly subtropical Rio Grande Valley in southern Texas, where in 1929, the Ruby Red grapefruit was discovered as a volunteer limb mutation on a pink grapefruit tree. This new variety was renown for its deep ruby red color, exceptionally sweet flavor, and superior quality. Today, most grapefruits are cultivated in Texas and Florida, with such varieties as Ruby Red and Star Red from Texas and Indian River and Orchid Island from Florida. Grapefruits are very high in vitamin C and fiber.

Grapefruits grow in clusters that hang from trees with glossy, dark green leaves. Because they are clustered, they resemble grapes, except that they are much larger. The three main varieties are the white, pink/red, and Star Ruby/Rio Red. All grapefruit have a similar tangy-sweet flavor and are exceptionally juicy.

When selecting a grapefruit, look for one that is round, heavy for its size, springy to the touch, has a skin that is smooth and thin, and exudes a lovely sweet fragrance. Wash grapefruit and store them in an open container in the refrigerator.

Grapefruit juice is delicious on its own but also combines nicely with oranges, apples, and other fruits. Before juicing, remove the skin but leave as much of the white pith as possible. Cut or tear the grapefruit into segments.

Lemon

The lemon was cultivated in India at least 2,500 years ago. It has an acidic flavor, but its skin contains an essential aromatic oil. This oval, yellow citrus fruit can range from small with a thin, smooth skin to large with a rough, thick skin. Although there are different varieties of lemons, it is very difficult to tell the difference between them. Lemons are a rich source of vitamin C.

When choosing a lemon, first identify those with a fine-textured skin, and then select a medium to large fruit that is firm and heavy for its size. The deeper yellow lemons are usually more mature and will have a less acidic flavor, while coarse-skinned lemons will yield less juice. Wash lemons and store them in the refrigerator.

Lemon juice is very sour when not mixed with other ingredients. Before juicing a lemon, remove the skin, leaving as much of the pith as possible. Cut the lemon into quarters or segments and combine with other fruits. It may be necessary to sweeten the juice with a little sugar.

Lime

The lime is a small aromatic fruit with a flavor similar to the lemon except that it is less acidic and more aromatic. It has a smooth, light to dark green skin and measures about 1½ inches in diameter. The lime is native to India and grows in most subtropical regions, such as Mexico and the West Indies. Limes are an excellent source of vitamin C.

To choose a lime with the most juice, look for a medium to large fruit that is firm and heavy for its size. Wash the lime and store it in the refrigerator.

Lime juice is very sour when used alone. Before juicing a lime, remove the skin, leaving as much of the pith as possible. Cut the lime in half or in segments and combine it with other fruits. It may be necessary to sweeten the juice with a little sugar.

Oranges

Fresh oranges are widely grown in California and Arizona and are available all year long. The two major varieties are the Valencias and navel. Two other varieties grown in the western states are the Cara Cara navel and the Moro orange (similar to the blood orange), both of which are available throughout the winter months. Oranges are very high in vitamin C.

When selecting an orange for the highest juice content, look for one that is heavy for its size and firm. Avoid an orange with a bruised skin because this may be a sign of fermentation, as well as oranges with a loose skin, indicating they may be dry. Although oranges can be stored at room temperature for a couple of days, their flavor is best when kept refrigerated. Wash oranges before storing them.

To juice an orange, remove the skin but leave as much of the white pith as possible. Cut or tear the orange into segments.

Blood Oranges   Blood oranges are very juicy and have a slightly sweet flavor with strawberry and raspberry overtones. They have a thin skin that is smooth and finely textured and does not peel as easy as some of the other varieties. These oranges are in season from December though the middle of May.

Moro Blood Oranges   These small to medium-size oranges have an orange skin covered with a red blush and a deep maroon interior. They are slightly tart in flavor with a hint of raspberry. Moros are available from December to May.

Navel Oranges   Navel oranges are easily identified by the navel (or button) formation on the end opposite the stem. Fruit specialists believe the navel is a smaller fruit attached to the main orange, which becomes visible after you peel the orange. Navel oranges are seedless, easy to peel, and very juicy. These oranges are available November though May.

Valencias Valencia oranges are late-ripening and are available from early summer through October. These small to medium-size oranges are an excellent choice for juicing. They usually have a thin skin and do not have many seeds.

Tangerines

Tangerines, also known as mandarins, are a close cousin of the orange. They have a light orange, smooth skin and are sweet in flavor. Comparing tangerines to oranges, tangerines are smaller and have a looser skin. However, any tangerine with a very loose, puffy skin should be avoided because this indicates that it is probably passed its prime. Always wash tangerines before storing them at room temperature or in the refrigerator. To juice a tangerine, remove the skin, leaving as much of the pith as possible. Cut or tear the tangerine into segments.

Clementines Clementines are members of the mandarin family. These glossy-skinned fruits are very petite yet firm. They are known for their tender and sweet flavor, as well as being virtually seedless and very juicy. Clementines are available from late November through April.

Dancy Tangerines Dancy tangerines are sometimes referred to as the "Christmas" tangerine in the United States because they are available in December and January. They have a reddish orange exterior and a deep orange interior. Their flavor is distinctively sweet-tart, and they have many seeds.

Honey Mandarins   Honey mandarins have a high sugar content, making them aromatic and richly sweet in flavor. This slightly flattened mandarin has a thin and glossy exterior and a very sweet and juicy flesh. Honey mandarins are available from mid-January though April.

Mineola Tangerines   Mineola tangerines are a cross between a Duncan grapefruit and a Dancy tangerine. This hybrid is sometimes referred to as a tangelo. They stand out from other tangerines because they are larger, have a deep, reddish exterior, and have a knoblike formation on one end. They are available from mid-December through April.

Satsuma Mandarins   Satsuma mandarins are the first variety to appear in the supermarket, from mid-October through December. Their skin and interior is bright orange, and they are sweet, very juicy, and virtually seedless.

Cranberries

The cranberry is a small, round, ruby-red, acidic fruit that grows wild on a vine in the marshes and bogs of northern Europe, and it is cultivated in the United States. They are available in November and December. Cranberries are rich in vitamin C.

When choosing cranberries, look for those that are plump, red, and firm. If you buy the prepackaged variety, wash them well just before you are ready to juice them, and remove any that are soft and mushy.

Because cranberry juice alone is very tart, it is best to combine it with the juice of a sweeter fruit. If necessary, add sugar to taste.

Grapes

Grapes are berries that grow in clusters on a woody vine. They are usually small, round, and smooth-skinned and range from black, blue, green, red, and golden, to purple. There are two main types of grapes: Old World or European and North American.

The grape is considered to be the most widely cultivated fruit in the world. Grapes were first cultivated about eight thousand years ago. In 1769, Spanish explorers established missions throughout California and planted a European grape variety, known as the mission. About 95 percent of all grapes grown today are European in origin. In the United States, these grapes are grown mainly in California, and their varieties are classified as wine, table, or raisin grapes. There are two main types of North American grapes: fox grapes and muscadine grapes, both of which can be eaten fresh or made into wine or jelly. Grapes are high in vitamin C.

When choosing grapes, look for those that are firm, well colored, and plump, and have a bloom, or a slight powder appearance. Avoid any that are soft and mushy or those that easily fall off the stem. Because grapes are heavily sprayed with chemicals, it is best to buy organic ones. Whether organic or not, grapes should be thoroughly washed. When dry, store them in the refrigerator for a few days.

Remove the grapes from the stem before placing them in the juicer.

Kiwifruit

The kiwifruit, or kiwi, is about the size of a plum and grows on a vine. It has a brown fuzzy skin and a luscious emerald-green pulp that surrounds a cluster of black seeds and has a sweet-sour taste. The kiwi originated in the 1600s in the Yangtze River valley in China and was called "Yangtao." In 1906, Yangtao seeds were sent to New Zealand, where the fruit was renamed Chinese gooseberry. In 1962, the Chinese gooseberry was shipped to the United States, where it was again renamed the "kiwifruit" in honor of New Zealand's famous national bird. Kiwi is high in vitamin C.

When choosing a kiwi, look for one that has a sweet aroma and is plump and firm yet will give slightly when pressed. Kiwi can be ripened at room temperature for three to five days. When ripe, store the kiwi in the refrigerator for a few days.

Kiwi juice is especially delicious when combined with the juice of other fruits. Cut the kiwifruit in half before adding to the juicer.

Mangoes

The mango was cultivated in India and the Malay Archipelago about four thousand years ago. In the 1700s and 1800s, European explorers introduced the fruit to other tropical areas. Mangoes were first raised in the United States sometime in the early 1900s.

The mango resembles a peach in appearance but is more elongated. It has a thin, leathery skin that can be yellow or red. The skin surrounds a very aromatic and juicy pulp and a hard inner pit. Mangoes are rich in beta-carotene and vitamins A and C.

When choosing a mango, look for one that is very fragrant, plump around the stem area, and gives slightly when pressed. Mangoes can also be ripened at room temperature. Wash them well before using.

To juice a mango, peel away the skin and remove the pit. Cut the mango into cubes or wedges just large enough to fit in the juicer.

Melons

Melons, surprisingly, are members of the cucumber family. They grow on vines that can be up to 7 feet long. There are two distinct types of melons: muskmelons and watermelons. In the muskmelon category are the summer melons, cantaloupe and muskmelon, and the winter melons include the casaba and honeydew. All melons are high in vitamin C.

When choosing a melon, look for one that is unblemished, firm, and free of any soft spots. Pick up a few melons and choose the one that is the heaviest for its size. Also, smell the stem end of the melon to see whether it has a fresh aroma. If it has no aroma, then the fruit is not ripe. Melons should be washed and refrigerated until ready to use.

I prefer to remove the skin before juicing a melon. However, the skin is loaded with nutrients, and you may choose to leave it on. Cut the melon in half, remove the seeds, and then cut the melon into wedges or cubes that are large enough to fit in your juicer.

Many different kinds of melons are available, but I will include descriptions of those that are most likely to appear in your local farmer's market or supermarket.

Cantaloupes

Cantaloupes are one of the most popular melons, possessing a hint of a sweet nutty flavor. The Eastern style is large with a soft, thick, and juicy interior, while the Western style is smaller, with a crunchier, firm interior that is not as aromatic. All cantaloupes are ripe when the skin under the netting appears a light golden color rather than green or orange and when the stem end has a good aroma.

Honeydew

The honeydew melon is large with a smooth, creamy yellow rind and a green interior. When the honeydew is ripe, it should be firm with a small amount of softness near the stem end and have a slight fruit aroma.

Watermelon

The large watermelon can be round or oblong. It has a thick, green rind and a deliciously sweet, red interior. Because the watermelon consists of 91 percent water, it is an ideal fruit to juice. Today, seedless watermelons are also available. These watermelons may contain some edible white seeds but are free of the hard black seeds.

Most watermelons are harvested between April and October. To test for ripeness, turn the watermelon over and look for any yellow color on the underside. Also, the rind should be void of any soft spots.

Papayas

The papaya has a smooth skin that can be green or greenish yellow. It surrounds a flesh that ranges from yellow-orange to salmon toned. It has a slightly elongated shape, similar to that of an avocado, and contains many edible seeds. Its flavor has been described as musky peachy-apricot. Papayas are an excellent source of vitamin C and beta-carotene.

When choosing a papaya, look for one that is heavy for its size and gives slightly when pressed. Also, the papaya should have a pleasant aroma. If the skin is spotted, this will not affect the flavor. Papayas are at their peak during May and June. Wash them before using.

To juice a papaya, first remove the skin and seeds and then cut the papaya into cubes or wedges just large enough to fit in the juicer.

Passion Fruit

The passion fruit is a round or egg-shaped fruit with a skin that is thick, waxy, hard, and wrinkled. It encloses an aromatic, jelly-like golden flesh filled with edible seeds and measures about 1½ to 3 inches wide. The New Zealand passion fruit is purple, and the Hawaiian passion fruit is yellow. All passion fruit have a musky sweet-tart flavor.

When choosing a passion fruit, look for one that is fragrant, shriveled, and rich in color. If the passion fruit has a smooth skin, you can ripen it at room temperature for a few days, turning the fruit occasionally. Wash the passion fruit and refrigerate it in an airtight plastic bag for a few days.

To juice a passion fruit, cut the fruit in half before adding it to the juicer.

Peaches and Nectarines

Peaches have been grown since prehistoric times and were first cultivated in China. They were later introduced into Europe and Persia. It is believed that the Spaniards brought peaches to the United States and Central and South America. The Spanish missionaries planted the first peach trees in California.

Numerous varieties of peaches are available, and they are broken down into rough classifications. One type of peach is the "freestone," so named because the pit separates easily from the peach. Another type is the "clingstone" because the pit is firmly attached to the fruit. Freestone peaches are most often found in the supermarket because they are easy to eat, while clingstone peaches are frequently canned. Peaches are available almost year-round and are a good source of vitamins A and C.

When choosing peaches, look for ones that are relatively firm with a fuzzy, creamy yellow skin, and a sweet aroma. The pink blush on the peach indicates its variety, not its ripeness. Avoid peaches with a wrinkled skin or those that are soft or blemished.

The peach should yield gently when touched. To ripen peaches, keep them at room temperature, out of direct sun, until the skin yields slightly to the touch. Once ripe, wash the peaches and store them in the refrigerator in a single layer for up to five days.

The nectarine is a smooth-skinned variety of the peach. Nectarines are high in vitamin C.

When choosing nectarines, look for those with bright red markings over a yellow skin. Avoid any with a wrinkled skin or those that are soft or bruised. The nectarine should yield gently to the touch and have a sweet aroma.

For juicing, remove the pit and cut the peach or nectarine into wedges just large enough to fit in your juicer.

Pears

Pear refers to the name of a tree of the rose family and its fruit. It is believed that pears were eaten by Stone Age people. However, the pears we are accustomed to eating were first cultivated in southeastern Europe and western Asia, as early as 2000 B.C. Pear trees were first planted in America in the early seventeenth century. Pears are a source of vitamin C and fiber.

Although pears are available year-round, they ripen better off the tree. This explains why they are often so hard when purchased at the supermarket. Many pears have stickers that tell you the stage of ripeness, such as "ready to eat" or "let me ripen for 2 days." Therefore, when choosing pears, look for ones that are firm and unblemished with a fresh aroma. To ripen them at home, place them in a brown paper bag at room temperature for a few days. Once ripe, wash the pears and refrigerate them from two to five days.

To make pear juice, cut the pear into wedges just large enough to fit in your juicer. Pear juice, alone is delicious, but it also combines well with the juice of most other fruit juices.

With the vast number of pear varieties (over three thousand), I will briefly discuss the four that are most often available.

Anjou

Anjou pears are large, oval shaped with a light green to yellow-green smooth, thin skin on the outside. They are available from October through June.

Bartlett

Bartlett pears are bell shaped and turn from green to yellow when ripe. There is also a red variety, which turns bright red when ripe. These aromatic pears are available from July through December.

Bosc

Bosc pears have a long neck and stem with a rough skin on the outside. They have a light rusted or cinnamon-colored skin and are available from August to May.

Comice

Comice pears are round with a short neck and stem. They are large and plump with a pale greenish yellow skin that sometimes has a hint of a blush. Comice pears are available from August through April.

Persimmons

Persimmons have been cultivated in China for centuries. They later spread to Korea and Japan. In the mid-1800s, the persimmon plant was introduced to California. Some persimmons are round, while others have an acorn shape, or they may be flattened or somewhat square. They range from light yellow-orange to dark orange-red. The whole fruit is edible except for the seed and calyx. They have a very sweet, fruity flavor when ripe but are exceptionally sour when unripe. Persimmons are rich in vitamin C.

When choosing a persimmon, a very good indication of its ripeness is a full color and a slightly wrinkled skin. In fact, the fruits that taste best are those that almost look spoiled.

To juice a persimmon, remove the seed and cut the fruit into quarters before adding it to the juicer.

Pineapples

Pineapples are a tropical fruit native to Central and South America. In 1493, Christopher Columbus discovered pineapples growing on the island of Guadeloupe and brought them back to

Spain. In the 1700s, it is reported that pineapples were grown in greenhouses throughout Europe. Pineapples are an excellent source of vitamin C.

When choosing a pineapple, look for one that has a fresh pineapple aroma and a crown with crisp, fresh-looking leaves and a brightly colored shell. Avoid any pineapples that have soft spots or are discolored. Wash the pineapple well.

To juice a pineapple, remove the crown. Cut the fruit, with skin and core, into spears or cubes before juicing.

Plums

Wild plums have been around for so long that they were gathered by our prehistoric ancestors. Later, it is believed that cultivated plum plants were introduced in ancient Rome from Damascus. Today, two hundred to three hundred varieties of plums are grown in the United States. They come in a wide range of colors, ranging from purple and red to yellow, green, and blue. The damson, which is small and oval and has a tart flavor, is the family to which several varieties of common garden plums belong. Plums are rich in vitamin C.

Choose a plum that has good color, is heavy for its size, and has a sweet fragrance. The fruit should yield slightly to pressure, especially close to the end stem. Avoid any plums that are too soft, have a shriveled skin, exhibit brown spots, or show any sign of leakage. If the plum is hard, it will ripen in a brown paper bag at room temperature after a few days. Wash plums well and store them in a single layer in the refrigerator for up to five days.

Plum juice is especially delicious when combined with the juice of other fruits. To juice a plum, cut it in half and remove the pit before adding it to the juicer.

Pomegranates

Pomegranates grow on a deciduous thorny shrub or small tree and is native to the semitropical region of Asia. They have a hard, red skin enclosing hundreds of edible fleshy seeds, each surrounded by a juicy, translucent pulp. Pomegranates are a source of potassium, fiber, and a little vitamin C.

When choosing a pomegranate, look for one with a thin, tough, unbroken skin. A medium-size pomegranate, about the size of an orange, will yield approximately ½ cup of juice.

Pomegranate juice is best combined with the juice of other fruits. To juice a pomegranate, the seeds and pulp must be carefully removed. Using a very sharp knife, carefully slice off the stem end of the fruit. Make four cuts through the skin, each starting at the exposed stem end and working the knife down to the opposite end. Break the fruit into quarters, and use your fingers to remove the seeds.

Raspberries

It is believed that red raspberries spread all over Europe and Asia in prehistoric times. Because these raspberries were so delicious growing wild, it was not until the 1600s that they were cultivated in Europe. The raspberries that are cultivated in North America originated from two groups: the red raspberry, which was native to Europe, and the wild red variety, which was native to North America. Raspberries are an excellent source of vitamin C, fiber, and potassium.

When choosing raspberries, it is always best to buy them when they are in season, which usually begins in late June and lasts four to six weeks. If you are fortunate enough to have a local berry farm, take advantage of it by visiting at the beginning of the season to get the best pick. Choose berries that are large and plump, bright, shiny, uniform in color, and free of mold. Avoid any raspberries that are mushy. Before refrigerating raspberries for up to one day, carefully go through the batch and discard any that show signs of spoilage. Wash the raspberries just before you are ready to use them.

Strawberries

The existence of strawberries dates as far back as 2,200 years ago. They are known to have grown wild in Italy in the third century and, by 1588, were discovered in Virginia by the first European settlers. Local Indians cultivated the strawberry as early as the mid-1600s, and by the middle of the nineteenth century, this fruit was widely grown in many parts of the country.

The strawberry grows on a plant very low to the ground on a stem in groups of three. As the fruit ripens, it changes from greenish white to a lush flame red. The strawberry does not have a skin but is actually covered by hundreds of tiny seeds. Strawberries are a rich source of vitamin C and fiber.

The best time to buy strawberries is in June and July when they are at their peak of juicy freshness. As with raspberries, if you are lucky enough to live near a strawberry farm, a "pick your own" day trip is a wonderful family outing as well as an excellent way to get the very best of the crop. Look for plump, firm, and deep-colored fruit with a bright green cap and a sweet aroma. Strawberries can be stored in a single layer in the refrigerator for up to two days and washed with their cap just before you are ready to use them.

To juice strawberries, place them in the juicer and process. Strawberry juice is delicious on its own but also combines well with the juice of most other fruit juices.

ABOUT ORGANIC FOODS

Most books on fruit and vegetable juicing stress the desirability of buying organic produce whenever possible. Every year in the United States, over a billion pounds of herbicides and pesticides are sprayed on crops to battle insects and weeds. While a small percentage of these toxic substances adheres to the targeted crops and is effective, the vast majority is unfortunately absorbed in our soil and water, resulting in a frightening potential health risk to humans.

Those of us who share in these concerns should consider buying organic produce, where it is available. Organic farming is based on a system of agriculture that maintains and replenishes soil fertility without the use of chemical fertilizers, in turn producing healthier plants that can naturally resist disease and insects without synthetic pesticides. In this system, should the pest population get out of control, insect predators, mating disruptions, traps, and barriers are introduced as a defense.

You can be confident that produce marked "certified organic" was grown according to strict uniform standards that are verified by independent state or private organizations. As part of the certification process, farm fields are inspected and soil and water periodically tested to assure that the farmer is meeting standards set by the federal government in the Organic Food Act of 1990. Only farms that meet these standards can be certified as organic. Even more strict federal guidelines governing organic certification have been proposed that would go beyond banning toxic pesticides by prohibiting genetic engineering, irradiation, and the use of sewage sludge.

While organic produce is a better alternative to eating fresh fruits and vegetables that have been heavily sprayed with pesticides and herbicides, there is no evidence that it is any more nutritious. However, organic produce often has a richer flavor as a result of having been cultivated in a more well-balanced soil.

Organic foods are most often available in natural food stores, health food sections of supermarkets, farmer's markets, and by mail from specialty retailers. Keep in mind that organic produce, like the nonorganic variety, should also be washed well and rinsed thoroughly under cold running water. A variety of biodegradable cleaners with explicit instructions are also available for this purpose.

CHAPTER 3

Selecting a Juicer

*N*ow that you have made the decision to join ranks with millions of other juice aficionados, I hope you will find this discussion of the different kinds of juicers helpful in selecting the model that best fits your needs and budget. However, I encourage you to visit an appliance or health food store and actually view the models they have available. By browsing, you will be best able to determine which model meets your needs and appreciate the different sizes and shapes of juicers so that you can determine which one would fit best on your counter space or in your cabinet. Another resource for gleaning valuable information on juicers is the Internet. Many manufacturers have sites that describe their individual product, and some provide a phone number so you can personally speak to a representative. Finally, *Consumer Reports* and other similar publications provide comparison quality ratings on a wide selection of juicers.

You should keep in mind certain basic features when choosing a juicer, including durability, ease of operation, convenience of cleaning, and noise production. The most important consideration is whether it produces high-quality juice and yield and will easily accept the type of produce you will be juicing. Lastly, review the length of the juicer's warranty. Once those criteria are covered, you are almost ready to reach for your checkbook. I hope the following list of the various juicers available will help you in your decision.

- **Centrifugal juicer**
  The centrifugal juicer consists of a straight-sided strainer basket with a grater or shredder disc on the bottom of the basket. When produce is inserted into the juicer, it hits the shredder disc at the bottom of the basket, which spins at 3,600 rpm (revolutions per minute). As the produce is being shredded, centrifugal action forces the pure juice through the thousands of side openings on the basket, while the pulp adheres to the sides of the basket.

  The centrifugal juicer is not a continuous juicer, because after it makes about 1 to 2 quarts of juice, it must be turned off and the pulp removed. This type of juicer works equally well with fruits and vegetables. Examples of centrifugal juicers are the Acme 6001 and the Omega 1000.

- **Centrifugal ejection juicer**
  The centrifugal ejection juicer is very similar to the centrifugal juicer except that the sides of the basket are slanted. This simple alteration allows the pulp to be ejected out of the machine into a collection basket or bin. Lining the basket with a plastic bag makes it easy to remove the contents. Another difference between the two juicers is that this variety spins at a higher speed of 6,300 rpm. This type of juicer is easy to operate and very easy to clean. Examples of centrifugal ejection juicers are the Juiceman II, L'equip 221, Miracle Ultra-Matic, and Omega 4000.

- **Masticating juicer**
  The masticating juicer has a powerful, slow-turning motor that grates then masticates or chews the fibers of fruits and vegetables, breaking up their cell walls and finally mechanically squeezing the resulting pulp to extract juice. This kind of juicer works best with vegetables. Because the slow-turning motor causes less oxidation of vegetables, this juicer produces a high-quality juice with excellent retention of most vitamins and nutrients. An example of a masticating model is the Champion Juicer.

- **Twin gear press**
  The twin gear press is the kind of juicer I personally prefer. It can juice vegetables and fruits, as well as wheatgrass. This juicer contains twin gears that turn at a low speed of 90 to 110 rpm. Produce is pushed through a

feed tube into the twin gears where it is first shredded and then squeezed. Juice flows out of one tube, and pulp is ejected out of another. Although this juicer can be used with fruits, it works best with vegetables because it relies on the fibrous cell walls to push the pulp through the machine. This juicer will produce the juice with the highest nutritional quality because the very slowly spinning gears minimize oxidation. Examples of the twin gear press are the Green Life Juice Extractor, Green Power Juice Extractor, and the Omega 8000 (the Omega will only make vegetable juice).

- **Wheatgrass juicer**
  A number of juicers are specially designed to extract wheatgrass juice. Manual wheatgrass juicers must be clamped on to a table or countertop before the wheatgrass is inserted into a feed tube. When you turn the crank, an auger exerts pressure on the blades of the wheatgrass and squeezes out the juice. Juice emerges from one opening while the pulp comes out of another. There are also electric wheatgrass juicers that have continuous pulp expulsion, are self-feeding, and are mounted on a self-contained base. Two popular manual wheatgrass juicers are the Miracle Manual Wheatgrass Juicer and the Back to Basics Manual Wheatgrass Juicer. Those who prefer electric wheatgrass juicers may want to consider either the Miracle (Exclusives-MJ550 or Professional-MJ475) or the Wheateena Marvel (Green or Red Label).

Once you have purchased your juicer, read the instructions that accompany it carefully. It is helpful to take the juicer apart once so you can become more familiar with its parts. You should also be certain you understand how to keep your juicer clean. Washing the appliance after each use prevents any of the pulp from hardening on the parts.

After you have familiarized yourself with your juicer, you can start on your exciting adventure into the wonderful world of juicing. I doubt that you'll ever want to turn back.

Back to Basics

Classic Juice Combinations

*T*he infinite number of fruit and vegetable juices that can be created with a juicer never ceases to amaze even veteran juicers. If your taste buds tend to lean toward sweeter foods, you will adore the endless number of fruit juices that can be made with a single fruit or a combination of two or more. Or, if you prefer zesty flavors, you are in for a big surprise when you taste how delicious a vegetable juice can be. If you don't belong to either party and like both sweet and zesty flavors, you will be delighted with the combination of fruit and vegetable juices that will simultaneously satisfy both tastes.

Because juice blends are so personal, I have only included a sampling of fruit and vegetable recipes in this chapter as an introduction to the different combinations that are possible. Many of the popular basic juices are ideal candidates for blending with some of the stronger-flavored vegetable juices, such as broccoli, green beans, cauliflower, or brussels sprouts, to name just a few. Don't hesitate to substitute any of your favorite fruits or vegetables for the ones I have suggested. The key is to experiment with different ingredients until you discover your favorite combinations. With fruit or vegetable in hand and your juicer ready to go, it is now up to you to unleash that creative spirit and put your own signature on the ultimate juice. (Since these drinks are so simple, I have not provided nutritional information for each combination; however, each of these recipes yields 1 serving and the nutritional information for each fruit and vegetable included in these drinks is listed in table 4.1 on page 60.)

APPLE ADVENTURES

You will be delighted with the variety of delicious juices you can create by combining an apple and any of your other favorite fruits. Almost any vegetable can also be mixed with this versatile fruit, with an equally pleasing result. These recipes are just a sampling of the endless number of apple juices you can enjoy; use them as a guide and have fun creating your favorites.

Table 4.1. Nutritional information for individual fruits and vegetables.

	Cals.	Cals. from fat	Fat (g)	Carb. (g)	Protein (g)	Fiber (g)	Calcium (mg)	Iron (mg)	Folic acid (mcg)	Mag. (mg)	Pot. (mg)	Beta Carotene (mcg)	Vit. A (mcg)	Vit. C (mg)	Vit. E (IU)
Apple	81	4	0.5	21	0.26	4	10	0.25	4	7	159	28	7	8	0.66
Apricot	17	1	0.14	4	0.49	0.85	5	0.19	3	3	105	550	92	4	0.47
Beet	52	2	0.21	12	2	3	19	0.97	133	28	395	15	5	6	0.54
Cabbage	227	22	2	49	13	21	427	5	390	136	2234	708	118	292	1
Cantaloupe	200	0	0	48	4	4	80	1	0	0	1120	11928	2000	192	0
Carrot	31	1	0.14	7	0.74	2	19	0.36	10	11	233	9843	2025	7	0.49
Celery	6	0.50	0.06	1	0.30	0.68	16	0.16	11	4	115	31	5	3	0.21
Cherry	5	0.59	0.07	1	0.08	0.16	1	0.03	0.29	0.75	15	8	1	0.48	0.01
Cranberry (½ cup)	23	0.85	0.10	6	0.19	2	3	0.10	0.81	2	34	14	2	6	0.07
Cucumber	39	4	0.39	8	2	2	42	0.78	39	33	433	379	63	16	0.36
Fennel	73	4	0.47	17	3	7	115	2	63	40	969	183	30	28	0
Ginger (1 piece)	2	0.16	0.02	0.38	0.04	0.05	0.45	0.01	0.28	1	10	0	0	0.13	0.01
Grape	4	0.26	0.03	1	0.03	0.05	0.55	0.01	0.20	0.30	9	2	0.35	0.54	0.05

Grapefruit	78	2	0.24	20	2	3	28	0.14	24	21	349	14	2	79	0.88
Honeydew	500	0	0	130	10	10	0	4	0	0	3100	600	100	270	0
Kiwi	50	5	0.50	12	1	2	30	0.36	0	0	240	30	5	72	0
Mango	135	5	0.56	35	1	4	21	0.27	29	19	323	4831	805	57	3
Orange	62	1	0.16	15	—	3	52	0.13	40	13	237	51	28	70	0.47
Peach	42	0.79	0.09	11	0.69	2	5	0.11	3	7	193	260	53	6	1
Pear	98	6	0.66	25	0.65	4	18	0.41	12	10	208	20	3	7	1
Pineapple	231	18	2	59	2	6	33	2	50	66	533	55	9	73	0.70
Plum	36	4	0.41	9	0.52	—	3	0.07	1	5	114	127	21	6	0.59
Raspberry	0.93	0.09	0.01	0.22	0.02	0.13	0.42	0.01	0.45	0.34	3	0.74	0.25	0.47	0.01
Red Bell Pepper	32	2	0.23	8	—	2	11	0.55	26	12	211	3675	678	226	1
Spinach	75	11	1	12	10	9	337	9	660	269	1897	13559	2285	96	10
Strawberry	4	0.40	0.04	0.84	0.07	0.28	2	0.05	2	1	20	2	0.36	7	0.03
Sweet Potato	137	4	0.39	32	2	4	29	0.77	18	13	265	15647	2608	30	0.54
Tangerine	50	5	0.50	15	1	3	40	0	0	0	180	0	0	30	0
Watermelon	1333	0	0	450	17	33	333	12	0	0	3833	9980	1667	250	0

Apple Juice

3 to 4 apples, cut into eighths

Place the apples in the juicer and process until juiced.

Apple and Beet Juice

4 apples, cut into eighths
½ beet with top

Alternate adding the apples and beet to the juicer and process until juiced.

Apple and Cranberry Juice

3 apples, cut into eighths
½ cup cranberries

Alternate adding the apples and cranberries to the juicer and process until juiced.

Apple and Kiwi Juice

2 apples, cut into eighths
3 kiwi, halved

Alternate adding the apples and kiwis to the juicer and process until juiced.

Apple and Orange Juice

2 apples, cut into eighths

2 oranges, peeled and cut into wedges

Alternate adding the apples and oranges to the juicer and process until juiced.

Apple and Peach Juice

2 apples, cut into eighths

1 peach, pitted and quartered

Alternate adding the apples and peach to the juicer and process until juiced.

Apple and Pear Juice

2 apples, cut into eighths

2 pears, cut into eighths

Alternate adding the apples and pears to the juicer and process until juiced.

Apple and Strawberry Juice (or Blueberry or Raspberry)

2 apples, cut into eighths

1 cup strawberries (or blueberries or raspberries)

Alternate adding the apples and berries to the juicer and process until juiced.

Apple and Tangerine Juice

2 apples, cut into eighths

1 tangerine, peeled and segmented

Alternate adding the apples and tangerine to the juicer and process until juiced.

CARROT CAPERS

Carrot juice has a naturally sweet flavor that blends well with most other vegetables, as well as with many fruits. Once you have tried some of these recipes, I am certain you will want to blaze a new path of discovery and create your own exciting carrot juice combos.

Carrot Juice

8 to 10 carrots, cut into 2- to 3-inch lengths

Place the carrots in the juicer and process until juiced.

Carrot and Apple Juice

6 carrots, cut into 2- to 3-inch lengths

1 apple, cut into eighths

Alternate adding the carrots and apple to the juicer and process until juiced.

Carrot and Beet Juice

4 carrots, cut into 2- to 3-inch lengths

½ beet with top

Alternate adding the carrots and beet to the juicer and process until juiced.

Carrot and Celery Juice

6 carrots, cut into 2- to 3-inch lengths

2 celery stalks, cut into 2- to 3-inch lengths

Alternate adding the carrots and celery to the juicer and process until juiced.

Carrot and Cucumber Juice

6 carrots, cut into 2- to 3-inch lengths

½ cucumber, cut into cubes or spears

Alternate adding the carrots and cucumber to the juicer and process until juiced.

Carrot and Ginger Juice

8 to 10 carrots, cut into 2- to 3-inch lengths

1 slice ginger, peeled and cut ¼ to ½-inch thick

Alternate adding the carrots and ginger to the juicer and process until juiced.

Carrot and Red Bell Pepper Juice

6 carrots, cut into 2- to 3-inch lengths

¼ red bell pepper, halved

Alternate adding the carrots and red pepper to the juicer and process until juiced.

Carrot and Sweet Potato Juice

6 carrots, cut into 2- to 3-inch lengths

1 cup cubed sweet potato

Alternate adding the carrots and sweet potato to the juicer and process until juiced.

CELERY CELEBRATIONS

The unique flavor of celery shines though pleasingly when it is combined with other fruits and vegetables to make a variety of distinctively flavored juices.

Celery and Apple Juice

2 celery stalks, cut into 2- to 3-inch lengths

1 apple, cut into eighths

Alternate adding the celery and apple to the juicer and process until juiced.

Celery and Cabbage Juice

3 celery stalks, cut into 2- to 3-inch lengths

⅛ wedge (4 ounces) cabbage, halved

Alternate adding the celery and cabbage to the juicer and process until juiced.

Celery and Fennel Juice

4 celery stalks, cut into 2- to 3-inch lengths

½ small fennel, halved

Alternate adding the celery and fennel to the juicer and process until juiced.

Celery and Pineapple Juice

2 celery stalks, cut into 2- to 3-inch lengths

1½ cups cubed pineapple

Alternate adding the celery and pineapple to the juicer and process until juiced.

CHERRIOTS OF FIRE

It will be a race to the finish line to see how many mouthwatering cherry juices you can create with this plump fruit that is bursting with delicious juice.

Cherry and Apricot Juice

2 cups Bing cherries, pitted

3 apricots, pitted and halved

Alternate adding the cherries and apricots to the juicer and process until juiced.

Cherry and Cranberry Juice

2 cups Bing cherries, pitted

1 cup cranberries

Alternate adding the cherries and cranberries to the juicer and process until juiced.

Cherry and Grapefruit Juice

2 cups Bing cherries, pitted

1 grapefruit, peeled and segmented

Alternate adding the cherries and grapefruit to the juicer and process until juiced.

Cherry and Pineapple Juice

1 cup Bing cherries, pitted

1 cup cubed pineapple

Alternate adding the cherries and pineapple to the juicer and process until juiced.

Cherry and Plum Juice

1 cup Bing cherries, pitted
2 plums, pitted and halved

Alternate adding the cherries and plums to the juicer and process until juiced.

FENNEL FANTASY

Once you have tasted any of these fennel juice recipes, I hope you will be inspired to create your own fantasy by combining fennel with some of your favorite fruits and vegetables.

Fennel and Apple Juice

2 apples, cut into eighths
1 small fennel bulb, halved

Alternate adding the apples and fennel to the juicer and process until juiced.

Fennel and Carrot Juice

6 carrots, cut into 2- to 3-inch lengths
1 small fennel, halved

Alternate adding the carrots and fennel to the juicer and process until juiced.

Fennel and Pear Juice

3 pears, cut into eighths

1 small fennel, halved

Alternate adding the pears and fennel to the juicer and process until juiced.

FRIDGE OVER BUBBLED WATER(MELON)

Hum along and you will be inspired to try watermelon and other members of the melon family as the basic ingredient for some fabulous juices.

Watermelon (Cantaloupe or Honeydew) Juice

3 cups cubed watermelon (cantaloupe or honeydew), rind removed and cut into cubes or spears

Place the melon in the juicer and process until juiced.

GRAPEFRUIT GRIPPERS

The strong flavor of grapefruit juice alone makes a refreshing and stimulating drink. When combined with some of your favorite fruits, you will find the flavor slightly tempered but still capable of adding some tang to your special blend.

Grapefruit and Apple Juice

1 grapefruit, peeled and segmented

2 apples, cut into eighths

Alternate adding the grapefruit and apples to the juicer and process until juiced.

Grapefruit and Apricot Juice

1 grapefruit, peeled and segmented

4 apricots, pitted and halved

Alternate adding the grapefruit and apricots to the juicer and process until juiced.

Grapefruit and Mango Juice

1 grapefruit, peeled and segmented

1 mango, pitted and cut into cubes

½ tablespoon superfine sugar (optional)

Alternate adding the grapefruit and mango to the juicer and process until juiced. Pour the juice into a glass and add the optional sugar. Blend well.

Grapefruit and Orange Juice

1 grapefruit, peeled and segmented

2 oranges, peeled and segmented

Alternate adding the grapefruit and oranges to the juicer and process until juiced.

Grapefruit and Pineapple Juice

1 grapefruit, peeled and segmented

1 cup cubed pineapple

Alternate adding the grapefruit and pineapple to the juicer and process until juiced.

GRAPE GUNS

Although grape juice is refreshingly delicious on its own, you will be pleased to discover how well it combines with most other fruits. Grapes are definitely a star fruit, and when you experiment with them in creating a variety of blended juices, you will find that they share the spotlight very graciously.

Grape Juice

3 cups grapes

Place the grapes in the juicer and process until juiced.

Grape and Apple Juice

2 cups grapes

2 apples, cut into eighths

Alternate adding the grapes and apples to the juicer and process until juiced.

Grape and Cherry Juice

2 cups grapes

1 cup Bing cherries, pitted

Alternate adding the grapes and cherries to the juicer and process until juiced.

Grape and Cranberry Juice

2 cups grapes

1 cup cranberries

Alternate adding the grapes and cranberries to the juicer and process until juiced.

Grape and Raspberry Juice

1½ cups grapes

1½ cups raspberries

Alternate adding the grapes and raspberries to the juicer and process until juiced.

MANGO MIRACLES

Mangoes are very sweet and combine well with most other fruits. Because they are fleshier than other fruits, you should add them slowly, one at a time, to the juicer to prevent it from getting clogged.

Mango and Apple Juice

1 mango, pitted and cut into cubes

2 apples, cut into eighths

Alternate adding the mango and apples to the juicer and process until juiced.

Mango and Pineapple Juice

1 mango, pitted and cut into cubes

1 cup cubed pineapple

Alternate adding the mango and pineapple to the juicer and process until juiced.

Mango and Strawberry Juice

1 mango, pitted and cut into cubes

12 strawberries

Alternate adding the mango and strawberries to the juicer and process until juiced.

Mango and Tangerine Juice

1 mango, pitted and cut into cubes

1 tangerine, peeled and segmented

Alternate adding the mango and tangerine to the juicer and process until juiced.

THE PEACH BOYS

If you favor sweet juices, you won't have to re-sort to California dreaming to satisfy your craving. Peaches combined with a variety of fruits yield a pleasingly sweet nectar.

Peach and Kiwi Juice

2 peaches, pitted and quartered

8 kiwi, halved

Alternate adding the peaches and kiwis to the juicer and process until juiced.

Peach and Strawberry Juice

2 peaches, pitted and quartered

8 strawberries

Alternate adding the peaches and strawberries to the juicer and process until juiced.

Peach and Tangerine Juice

2 peaches, pitted and quartered

1 tangerine, peeled and segmented

Alternate adding the peaches and tangerine to the juicer and process until juiced.

PEAR PRODUCTIONS

The distinct flavor of pear adds a delicate sweetness to a juice when combined with other fruits and some vegetables.

Pear and Cherry Juice

2 pears, cut into eighths

1 cup Bing cherries, pitted

Alternate adding the pears and cherries to the juicer and process until juiced.

Pear and Grapefruit Juice

2 pears, cut into eighths

½ grapefruit, peeled and segmented

Alternate adding the pears and grapefruit to the juicer and process until juiced.

Pear and Raspberry Juice

2 pears, cut into eighths

1 cup raspberries

Alternate adding the pears and raspberries to the juicer and process until juiced.

PINEAPPLE PURSUITS

Once you've enjoyed the ultimate sweetness of fresh pineapple juice, you will find it hard to go back to the canned variety. A pineapple that is freshly juiced yields a glass filled with a richly flavored foam and juice that has no equal. And just imagine the variety of deliciously frothy juices you will be able to create when pineapple is combined with other fruits and vegetables.

Pineapple Juice

3 cups cubed pineapple

Place the pineapple in the juicer and process until juiced.

Pineapple and Apple Juice

1½ cups cubed pineapple

1 apple, cut into eighths

Alternate adding the pineapple and apple to the juicer and process until juiced.

Pineapple and Apricot Juice

1½ cups cubed pineapple

2 apricots, pitted and halved

Alternate adding the pineapple and apricots to the juicer and process until juiced.

Pineapple and Grapefruit Juice

1½ cups cubed pineapple

½ grapefruit, peeled and segmented

Alternate adding the pineapple and grapefruit to the juicer and process until juiced.

Pineapple and Orange Juice

1½ cups cubed pineapple

1 orange, peeled and segmented

Alternate adding the pineapple and orange to the juicer and process until juiced.

Pineapple and Strawberry Juice

1½ cups cubed pineapple

8 strawberries

Alternate adding the pineapple and strawberries to the juicer and process until juiced.

Pineapple and Tangerine Juice

1 ½ cups cubed pineapple

2 tangerines, peeled and segmented

Alternate adding the pineapple and tangerines to the juicer and process until juiced.

SPINACH HARLEM

You won't be able to stop singing the praises of spinach after sampling some of these recipes. We all know how delicious spinach is when made into a vegetable side dish, salad, or a sensational dip. But when made into a juice, this green delight reaches new dimensions.

Spinach and Apple Juice

2 apples, cut into eighths

1 ½ cups packed spinach

Alternate adding the apples and spinach to the juicer and process until juiced.

Spinach and Carrot Juice

6 carrots, cut into 2- to 3-inch lengths

1 ½ cups packed spinach

Alternate adding the carrots and spinach to the juicer and process until juiced.

Spinach and Celery Juice

4 celery stalks, cut into 2- to 3-inch lengths

1 ½ cups packed spinach

Alternate adding the celery and spinach to the juicer and process until juiced.

Spinach and Red Pepper Juice

1 ½ cups packed spinach

¼ red pepper, halved

Alternate adding the spinach and red pepper to the juicer and process until juiced.

CHAPTER 5

Power Juices
for Your Health

A word of explanation is needed about this chapter devoted to healthful juices. Since fresh juices are virtually fat-free, low in calories, and loaded with nutrients, how can these remarkable liquids be made more health-filled for you? Many of us have discovered healthful herbs, extracts, and power boosters that can be added to our diets. Adding these supplements to a glass of fresh juice is an ideal way of reaping their health-enhancing benefits, in addition to the basic healthful effects of drinking fresh juice. Better yet, these additives almost never appreciably change the delicious taste of juice.

In addition to common supplements, wheatgrass and barley grass are also gaining in popularity because of the cornucopia of nutrients they contain and their energy-enhancing

qualities. Unfortunately, barley grass is not read-
ily available where I live, but you will be delighted to sample the many other recipes I have
provided that include wheatgrass. With the
more than thirty health-enhanced recipes in this
chapter, such as Ross Pear-Oh, The Lime of
Your Life, and Pleasure to Wheat You!, several
options here should satisfy your desire for a tall
glass of vitality.

Apple Mac'n Nosh

Click on to this juice and you will enter the next best experience to being in cyberspace.

1 SERVING

1 apple, cut into eighths

2 carrots, cut into 2- to 3-inch lengths

1 celery stalk, cut into 2- to 3-inch lengths

½ cucumber, cut into cubes or spears

½ cup packed spinach

Ginseng, as desired or according to specific brand label recommendations

Alternate adding the apple, carrots, celery, cucumber, and spinach to the juicer, and process until juiced. Pour the juice into a glass, and add the ginseng. Mix well. Garnish the rim of the glass with a Cucumber Wheel (page 211), if desired.

Calories	173	Calcium	100 mg
Calories from fat	10	Iron	2 mg
Total fat	1 g	Vitamin A	4195 mcg
Carbohydrates	42 g	Beta Carotene	20533 mcg
Protein	3 g	Vitamin K	276 mcg
Fiber	10 g	Potassium	1039 mg

Banana Koursinov-Apple

Sample this delicious juice, and in no time, you'll be "Russian" to the kitchen to serve some later.

1 SERVING

2 apples, cut into eighths

1 banana, peeled and cut into fourths

Ginseng, as desired or according to specific brand label recommendations

Add the apples to the juicer, and process until juiced. Place the banana in a blender; mix until pureed. Add the juice and ginseng to the blender, and mix until well blended. Pour the juice into a glass, and garnish the rim with a slice of lemon, if desired.

Calories	271	Calcium	26 mg
Calories from fat	14	Iron	0.86 mg
Total fat	2 g	Magnesium	48 mg
Carbohydrates	70 g	Potassium	78 mg
Protein	2 g	Folic acid	30 mcg
Fiber	10 g	Vitamin C	26 mg

Beet It!

The combination of piquant flavors in this juice is a real thriller!

1 SERVING

½ beet with top

1 tablespoon mint leaves

1 slice ginger, peeled and cut ¼- to ½-inch thick

1 to 2 ounces wheatgrass

1 clove garlic

1 orange, peeled and segmented

½ small lemon, peeled

Alternate adding half the beet, mint, ginger, wheatgrass, and garlic to the juicer, then the orange and lemon, followed by the remaining ingredients; process until juiced. Pour the juice into a glass, and garnish the rim with a slice of lemon, if desired.

Calories	111	Calcium	114 mg
Calories from fat	3	Iron	2 mg
Total fat	0.38 g	Beta Carotene	1272 mcg
Carbohydrates	26 g	Vitamin C	102 mg
Protein	4 g	Magnesium	51 mg
Fiber	6 g	Potassium	617 mg

Carrot Cold Buster

To combat a cold coming on or, better yet, to prevent one, this is the ideal juice for a healthy and delicious dose of vitamin C.

1 SERVING

2 carrots, cut into 2- to 3-inch lengths

1 apple, cut into eighths

⅔ cup cubed jicama

1 tablespoon vitamin C powder, or according to
   specific brand label recommendations

Alternate adding the carrots, apple, and jicama to the juicer, and process until juiced. Pour the juice into a glass, and add the vitamin C powder. Mix well. Garnish the rim of the glass with a slice of lemon, if desired.

Calories	174	Calcium	58 mg
Calories from fat	8	Iron	1 mg
Total fat	0.84 g	Vitamin C	37 mg
Carbohydrates	43 g	Vitamin K	216 mcg
Protein	2 g	Magnesium	38 mg
Fiber	12 g	Potassium	744 mg

Carrot Kiss

Do you remember your first kiss? With a generous dose of gingko biloba in this stimulating glassful, you won't forget your last one.

1 SERVING

2 carrots, cut into 2- to 3-inch lengths

1 celery stalk, cut into 2- to 3-inch lengths

8 sprigs of parsley

1 slice ginger, peeled and cut ¼- to ½-inch thick

2 plum tomatoes, halved

Gingko biloba, as desired or according to specific
   brand label recommendations

Alternate adding half the carrots, celery, parsley, and ginger to the juicer, then the tomatoes, followed by the remaining ingredients; process until juiced. Pour the juice into a glass, and add the gingko. Mix well. Garnish with a sprig of parsley, if desired.

Calories	99	Calcium	72 mg
Calories from fat	7	Iron	2 mg
Total fat	0.82 g	Vitamin C	51 mg
Carbohydrates	23 g	Folic acid	62 mcg
Protein	3 g	Magnesium	45 mg
Fiber	7 g	Potassium	910 mg

Eight Days a Wheat

With the energizing jolt from this wheatgrass upper, you'll feel fab every day of the week.

1 SERVING

4 carrots, cut into 2- to 3-inch lengths

1 celery stalk, cut into 2- to 3-inch lengths

8 sprigs of parsley

1 to 2 ounces wheatgrass

1 clove garlic

1 cup cherry tomatoes

Alternate adding half the carrots, celery, parsley, wheatgrass, and garlic to the juicer, then the tomatoes, followed by the remaining half of the ingredients; process until juiced. Pour the juice into a glass, and garnish with a celery stalk with leaves, if desired.

Calories	178	Calcium	118 mg
Calories from fat	11	Iron	3 mg
Total fat	1 g	Vitamin C	73 mg
Carbohydrates	40 g	Vitamin K	427 mcg
Protein	6 g	Magnesium	69 mg
Fiber	11 g	Potassium	1432 mg

Elvis Parsley Cocktail

This savory juice is the King! One taste and you'll be swiveling your hips in delight.

1 SERVING

4 carrots, cut into 2- to 3-inch lengths

8 sprigs of parsley

1 slice ginger, peeled and cut ¼- to ½-inch thick

1 tablespoon bee pollen, or according to specific
   brand label recommendations

Alternate adding the carrots, parsley, and ginger to the juicer, and process until juiced. Pour the juice into a glass, and add the bee pollen. Mix well. Garnish with a sprig of parsley, if desired.

Calories	157	Calcium	97 mg
Calories from fat	10	Iron	2 mg
Total fat	1 g	Vitamin C	42 mg
Carbohydrates	34 g	Vitamin K	418 mcg
Protein	5 g	Magnesium	53 mg
Fiber	10 g	Potassium	1005 mg

Eye Opener

Drinking a jolt-filled apple, tangerine, and wheat-grass juice every morning is a great way to start the day.

1 SERVING

2 apples, cut into eighths

1 tangerine, peeled and segmented

1 to 2 ounces wheatgrass

Alternate adding the apples, tangerine, and wheat-grass to the juicer, and process until juiced. Pour the juice into a glass, and garnish the rim with a slice of lemon, if desired.

Calories	210	Calcium	31 mg
Calories from fat	10	Iron	0.94 mg
Total fat	1 g	Vitamin C	45 mg
Carbohydrates	53 g	Folic acid	25 mcg
Protein	2 g	Magnesium	24 mg
Fiber	9 g	Potassium	449 mg

Gingko Garden of Eden

With its dollop of gingko biloba, you'll never forget this interesting juice, laden with a garden full of vegetables and one forbidden fruit.

1 SERVING

1 apple, cut into eighths

2 celery stalks, cut into 2- to 3-inch lengths

½ cucumber, cut into cubes or spears

¼ red bell pepper, halved

1 clove garlic

Gingko biloba, as desired or according to specific
 brand label recommendations

Alternate adding the apple, celery, cucumber, red pepper, and garlic to the juicer, and process until juiced. Pour the juice into a glass, and add the gingko. Mix well. Garnish the rim of the glass with a Cucumber Wheel (page 211), if desired.

Calories	126	Calcium	7 mg
Calories from fat	8	Iron	1 mg
Total fat	0.88 g	Vitamin C	79 mg
Carbohydrates	31 g	Folic acid	52 mcg
Protein	2 g	Magnesium	36 mg
Fiber	7 g	Potassium	670 mg

Ginseng in the Rain

Even if you haven't inherited a dancing Gene, you'll be twirling your umbrella and tapping your feet after one glassful of this stimulating elixir.

1 SERVING

1 cup raspberries

1 cup cubed cantaloupe

1 apple, cut into eighths

Ginseng, as desired or according to specific brand label recommendations

Alternate adding the raspberries, cantaloupe, and apple to the juicer, and process until juiced. Pour the juice into a glass, and add the ginseng. Mix well. Garnish with Berries on a Skewer (page 210), if desired.

Calories	198	Calcium	54 mg
Calories from fat	15	Iron	1 mg
Total fat	2 g	Vitamin C	106 mg
Carbohydrates	49 g	Folic acid	63 mcg
Protein	3 g	Magnesium	47 mg
Fiber	13 g	Potassium	840 mg

The Grapefruit Show on Earth!

No clowning around—if I said this drink wasn't great, I'd be "lion"!

1 SERVING

1 grapefruit, peeled and segmented

1 cup cubed pineapple

1 to 2 ounces wheatgrass

Alternate adding the grapefruit, pineapple, and wheatgrass to the juicer, and process until juiced. Pour the juice into a glass, and garnish with a wedge of pineapple, if desired.

Calories	164	Calcium	39 mg
Calories from fat	8	Iron	1 mg
Total fat	0.90 g	Vitamin C	106 mg
Carbohydrates	40 g	Folic acid	40 mcg
Protein	3 g	Magnesium	43 mg
Fiber	4 g	Potassium	524 mg

Laura's Lime Wheatgrass Juice

My daughter Laura created this recipe. It's easy to prepare and packs a punch for a busy and demanding lifestyle.

1 SERVING

2 apples, cut into eighths

1 lime, peeled and halved

1 to 2 ounces wheatgrass

Alternate adding the apples, lime, and wheatgrass to the juicer, and process until juiced. Pour the juice into a glass, and garnish the rim with a slice of lime, if desired.

Calories	193	Calcium	41 mg
Calories from fat	10	Iron	1 mg
Total fat	1 g	Vitamin C	39 mg
Carbohydrates	50 g	Folic acid	60 mcg
Protein	2 g	Magnesium	18 mg
Fiber	9 g	Potassium	386 mg

The Lime of Your Life

Don't let a cold get you down. Drink this vitamin C–packed juice and get feeling good again.

1 SERVING

4 limes, peeled and halved

1 cup sparkling mineral water

2 tablespoons superfine sugar, or to taste

1 tablespoon vitamin C powder, or according to specific brand label recommendations

Place the limes in the juicer, and process until juiced. Transfer the juice to a blender (or covered shaker); add the water, sugar, and vitamin C powder, and mix until well blended. Pour the juice into a glass, and garnish the rim with a slice of lime, if desired.

Calories	177	Calcium	89 mg
Calories from fat	5	Iron	2 mg
Total fat	0.54 g	Vitamin C	78 mg
Carbohydrates	53 g	Folic acid	22 mcg
Protein	7 g	Magnesium	16 mg
Fiber	8 g	Potassium	274 mg

Orange Sniffle Stifler

Got a cold? Want to feel better? With a combination of echinacea, bee pollen, and wheatgrass, this healthful potion will help you rebound in a hurry.

1 SERVING

2 oranges, peeled and segmented

1 to 2 ounces wheatgrass

1 tablespoon bee pollen, or according to specific brand label recommendations

Echinacea, as desired or according to specific brand label recommendations

Alternate adding the oranges and wheatgrass to the juicer, and process until juiced. Pour the juice into a glass, and add the bee pollen and echinacea. Mix well. Garnish the rim of the glass with an Orange Wheel (page 211), if desired.

Calories	161	Calcium	112 mg
Calories from fat	7	Iron	1 mg
Total fat	0.76 g	Beta Carotene	102 mcg
Carbohydrates	36 g	Vitamin C	147 mg
Protein	6 g	Folic acid	79 mcg
Fiber	7 g	Potassium	494 mg

Outrageously Orange Cold Blaster

The combination of echinacea and vitamin C not only is a potent cold fighter but also has a delightfully refreshing citrus flavor.

1 SERVING

1 orange, peeled and segmented

½ grapefruit, peeled and segmented

8 strawberries

1 tablespoon vitamin C, or according to specific brand label recommendations

Echinacea, as desired or according to specific brand label recommendations

Alternate adding the orange, grapefruit, and strawberries to the juicer, and process until juiced. Pour the juice into a glass, and add the vitamin C powder and echinacea. Mix well. Garnish the rim of the glass with a strawberry slice, if desired.

Calories	129	Calcium	80 mg
Calories from fat	6	Iron	0.57 mg
Total fat	0.63 g	Beta Carotene	73 mcg
Carbohydrates	32 g	Vitamin C	163 mg
Protein	3 g	Folic acid	68 mcg
Fiber	7 g	Potassium	571 mg

Perfect Pear

Most people put two things together and call it a pair. But why limit it to two when you can use four ingredients to make this "pear".

1 SERVING

1 Asian pear, peeled and cut into eighths

1 tangerine, peeled and segmented

1 cup cubed pineapple

Ginseng, as desired or according to specific brand label recommendations

Alternate adding the Asian pear, tangerine, and pineapple to the juicer, and process until juiced. Pour the juice into a glass, and add the ginseng. Mix well. Garnish with a wedge of pineapple, if desired.

Calories	164	Calcium	27 mg
Calories from fat	10	Iron	0.66 mg
Total fat	1 g	Beta Carotene	482 mcg
Carbohydrates	42 g	Vitamin C	54 mg
Protein	2 g	Folic acid	43 mcg
Fiber	8 g	Potassium	454 mg

Persimmon, Orange, and Kiwi Kiss

This drink won't turn a frog into a prince, but it is a refreshing juice that you will fall in love with.

1 SERVING

1 persimmon, peeled and quartered

1 orange, peeled and segmented

4 kiwis, halved

¼ cup sparkling apple cider

Gingko biloba, as desired or according to specific brand label recommendations

Alternate adding the persimmon, orange, and kiwis to the juicer, and process until juiced. Pour the juice into a glass, and add the cider and gingko. Mix well. Garnish the rim of the glass with a slice of kiwi, if desired.

Calories	327	Calcium	181 mg
Calories from fat	21	Iron	2 mg
Total fat	2 g	Beta Carotene	219 mcg
Carbohydrates	74 g	Vitamin C	379 mg
Protein	5 g	Magnesium	70 mg
Fiber	14 g	Potassium	1370 mg

Pleasure to Wheat You!

You'll be happy to introduce your friends to this wonderfully healthful and stimulating drink.

1 SERVING

2 carrots, cut into 2- to 3-inch lengths

1 celery stalk, cut into 2- to 3-inch lengths

1 apple, cut into eighths

1 to 2 ounces wheatgrass

½ cup cubed pineapple

Alternate adding half the carrots, celery, apple, and wheatgrass to the juicer, then the pineapple, followed by the remaining half of the ingredients; process until juiced. Pour the juice into a glass, and garnish with a wedge of pineapple, if desired.

Calories	198	Calcium	70 mg
Calories from fat	10	Iron	2 mg
Total fat	1 g	Beta Carotene	19755 mcg
Carbohydrates	48 g	Vitamin K	216 mcg
Protein	3 g	Magnesium	44 mg
Fiber	10 g	Potassium	826 mg

Popeye's Potion

The spinach and wheatgrass in this juice really pack a punch!

1 SERVING

½ cup packed spinach

3 asparagus spears, halved

2 carrots, cut into 2- to 3-inch lengths

1 celery stalk, cut into 2- to 3-inch lengths

1 to 2 ounces wheatgrass

1 plum tomato, halved

Alternate adding half the spinach, asparagus, carrots, celery, and wheatgrass to the juicer, then the tomato, followed by the remaining half of the ingredients; process until juiced. Pour the juice into a glass, and garnish with a celery stalk with leaves, if desired.

Calories	106	Calcium	83 mg
Calories from fat	6	Iron	2 mg
Total fat	0.68 g	Beta Carotene	20705 mcg
Carbohydrates	23 g	Folic acid	131 mcg
Protein	5 g	Vitamin K	292 mcg
Fiber	7 g	Potassium	932 mg

Ross Pear-Oh

You'll get a Texas-size jolt from this fruit and wheatgrass combination.

1 SERVING

1 pear, cut into eighths

1 cup cubed pineapple

1 to 2 ounces wheatgrass

Alternate adding the pear, pineapple, and wheatgrass to the juicer, and process until juiced. Pour the juice into a glass, and garnish with a Pineapple, Banana, and Cherry Charmer (page 216), if desired.

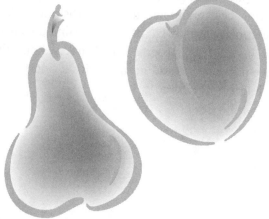

Calories	184	Calcium	29 mg
Calories from fat	12	Iron	1 mg
Total fat	1 g	Beta Carotene	38 mcg
Carbohydrates	45 g	Vitamin C	34 mg
Protein	2 g	Magnesium	32 mg
Fiber	6 g	Potassium	383 mg

Shakesparagus in Love

This invigorating juice can inspire sonnets that would melt the heart of the great bard himself.

1 SERVING

6 asparagus spears, halved

4 carrots, cut into 2- to 3-inch lengths

2 celery stalks, cut into 2- to 3-inch lengths

1 to 2 ounces wheatgrass

Alternate adding the asparagus, carrots, celery, and wheatgrass to the juicer, and process until juiced. Pour the juice into a glass, and garnish the rim with a Cucumber Wheel (page 211), if desired.

Calories	169	Calcium	130 mg
Calories from fat	8	Iron	3 mg
Total fat	0.85 g	Beta Carotene	39764 mcg
Carbohydrates	37 g	Folic acid	186 mcg
Protein	7 g	Vitamin K	456 mcg
Fiber	12 g	Potassium	1422 mg

Some Like It Hot, Hot, Hot!

The red chile makes this juice very hot. If you prefer less heat, halve the chile or eliminate it. The juice remains a delicious celebration of savory flavors.

1 SERVING

2 carrots, cut into 2- to 3-inch lengths

1 celery stalk, cut into 2- to 3-inch lengths

½ small sweet potato, cubed

8 sprigs of parsley

1 red chile

1 clove garlic

½ cucumber, cut into cubes or spears

2 plum tomatoes, halved

Ginseng, as desired or according to specific brand label recommendations

Alternate adding half the carrots, celery, sweet potato, parsley, chile, and garlic to the juicer, then the cucumber and tomatoes, followed by

Calories	208	Calcium	121 mg
Calories from fat	12	Iron	3 mg
Total fat	1 g	Beta Carotene	31050 mcg
Carbohydrates	47 g	Vitamin C	184 mg
Protein	6 g	Vitamin K	216 mcg
Fiber	11 g	Potassium	1414 mg

the other half of the ingredients; process until juiced. Pour the juice into a glass, and add the ginseng. Blend well. Garnish the rim of the glass with a Cucumber Wheel (page 211), if desired.

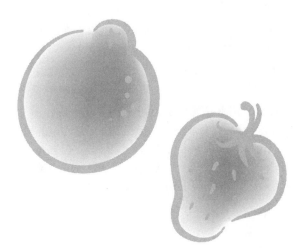

Strawberry Fields Forever . . . A Cold Never!

Your cold will be joining Lucy in the sky with diamonds, thanks to this juice.

1 SERVING

8 large strawberries

½ lemon, peeled and halved

1 tablespoon vitamin C powder, or according to specific brand label recommendations

½ tablespoon honey

Alternate adding the strawberries and lemon to the juicer, and process until juiced. Pour the juice into a glass, and add the vitamin C powder and honey. Mix well. Garnish the rim of the glass with a slice of lemon, if desired.

Calories	69	Calcium	22 mg
Calories from fat	4	Iron	0.58 mg
Total fat	0.44 g	Vitamin C	70 mg
Carbohydrates	18 g	Folic acid	20 mcg
Protein	0.94 g	Magnesium	12 mg
Fiber	3 g	Potassium	205 mg

Strawberry Forget-Me-Not

There will be no forgetting after a glassful of this gingko-fortified strawberry sensation.

1 SERVING

1 cup strawberries

1 cup raspberries

1 tangerine, peeled and segmented

1 small lime, peeled and halved

⅓ cup sparkling apple cider

1 to 2 teaspoons superfine sugar, or to taste

Gingko biloba, as desired or according to specific
    brand label recommendations

Place the strawberries, raspberries, tangerine, and lime in the juicer, and process until juiced. Pour the juice into a glass, and add the apple cider, sugar, and gingko. Mix well. Garnish with Berries on a Skewer (page 210), if desired.

Calories	210	Calcium	86 mg
Calories from fat	14	Iron	2 mg
Total fat	2 g	Beta Carotene	539 mcg
Carbohydrates	53 g	Vitamin C	158 mg
Protein	3 g	Folic acid	80 mcg
Fiber	16 g	Potassium	11 mg

To Bee or Not to Bee

This is a simple question to answer after one sip of this energizing juice.

1 SERVING

½ small beet with top

2 carrots, cut into 2- to 3-inch lengths

2 celery stalks, cut into 2- to 3-inch lengths

1 tablespoon bee pollen, or according to specific brand label recommendations

Alternate adding the beet, carrots, and celery to the juicer, and process until juiced. Pour the juice into a glass, and add the bee pollen. Mix well. Garnish with a celery stalk with leaves, if desired.

Calories	127	Calcium	123 mg
Calories from fat	8	Iron	3 mg
Total fat	0.92 g	Folic acid	92 mcg
Carbohydrates	27 g	Vitamin K	210 mcg
Protein	5 g	Magnesium	68 mg
Fiber	9 g	Potassium	1023 mg

Vitamin C Spree

With citrus plus added vitamin C, you'll be in antioxidant heaven with this stimulating juice.

2 SERVINGS

1 lemon, peeled and halved

1 orange, peeled and segmented

1½ cups cubed pineapple

2 teaspoons superfine sugar, or to taste

2 tablespoons vitamin C powder, or according to specific brand label recommendations

Alternate adding the lemon, orange, and pineapple to the juicer, and process until juiced. Pour the juice into a glass, and add the sugar and vitamin C powder. Mix well. Garnish the rim of the glass with a slice of lemon, if desired.

Calories	112	Calcium	42 mg
Calories from fat	6	Iron	0.67 mg
Total fat	0.67 g	Vitamin C	68 mg
Carbohydrates	29 g	Folic acid	35 mcg
Protein	1 g	Magnesium	25 mg
Fiber	4 g	Potassium	290 mg

We All Live in a Yellow Tangerine

All together now—this drink is a wonderful way to start any magical tour!

1 SERVING

1 tangerine, peeled and segmented

1 cup grapes

1 kiwi, halved

½ cup cubed pineapple

1 to 2 ounces wheatgrass

Alternate adding the tangerine, grapes, kiwi, pineapple, and wheatgrass to the juicer, and process until juiced. Pour the juice into a glass, and garnish the rim with a slice of kiwi, if desired.

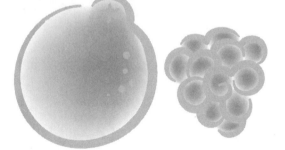

Calories	250	Calcium	64 mg
Calories from fat	17	Iron	1 mg
Total fat	2 g	Beta Carotene	581 mcg
Carbohydrates	59 g	Vitamin C	132 mg
Protein	4 g	Magnesium	44 mg
Fiber	7 g	Potassium	762 mg

Wheatgrass Combo Ecstasy

Once you have experienced the effect of this invigorating creation, you will join the ranks of millions of other loyal enthusiasts for this power-packed grass.

1 SERVING

4 carrots, cut into 2- to 3-inch lengths

2 celery stalks, cut into 2- to 3-inch lengths

1 cup packed spinach leaves

½ small beet with top

1 to 2 ounces wheatgrass

Alternate adding the carrots, celery, spinach, beet, and wheatgrass to the juicer, and process until juiced. Pour the juice into a glass, and garnish the rim with a Cucumber Wheel (page 211), if desired.

Calories	177	Calcium	184 mg
Calories from fat	8	Iron	4 mg
Total fat	0.85 g	Folic acid	170 mcg
Carbohydrates	39 g	Vitamin K	539 mcg
Protein	7 g	Magnesium	108 mg
Fiber	13 g	Potassium	1636 mg

Wheatgrass Hopper

Let's go to the hop(per). Oh baby, this refreshing drink is the perfect pick-me-up at any time of the day.

1 SERVING

2 cups cubed pineapple

1 to 2 ounces wheatgrass

Alternate adding the pineapple and wheatgrass to the juicer, and process until juiced. Pour the juice into a glass, and garnish with a Fruit Skewer (page 212), if desired.

Calories	162	Calcium	22 mg
Calories from fat	12	Iron	2 mg
Total fat	1 g	Vitamin C	51 mg
Carbohydrates	39 g	Folic acid	33 mcg
Protein	2 g	Magnesium	43 mg
Fiber	4 g	Potassium	350 mg

The Wheatgrass Is Always Greener

Spinach, asparagus, and celery add a healthful dose of green to this wheatgrass energizer.

1 SERVING

½ cup packed spinach

3 asparagus spears, halved

2 carrots, cut into 2- to 3-inch lengths

1 celery stalk, cut into 2- to 3-inch lengths

½ apple, quartered

1 to 2 ounces wheatgrass

1 plum tomato, halved

Alternate adding half the spinach, asparagus, carrots, celery, apple, and wheatgrass to the juicer, then the tomato, followed by the remaining ingredients; process until juiced. Pour the juice into a glass, and garnish the rim with a Cucumber Wheel (page 211), if desired.

Calories	146	Calcium	86 mg
Calories from fat	8	Iron	2 mg
Total fat	0.93 g	Folic acid	133 mcg
Carbohydrates	33 g	Vitamin K	295 mcg
Protein	5 g	Magnesium	57 mg
Fiber	9 g	Potassium	1012 mg

Wheatgrass Jolt

If you are looking for a special juice to get you going in the morning—or any time of the day—this is the one for you.

1 SERVING

4 carrots, cut into 2- to 3-inch lengths

1 celery stalk, cut into 2- to 3-inch lengths

1 cup red leaf lettuce

8 sprigs of parsley

1 to 2 ounces wheatgrass

Alternate adding the carrots, celery, lettuce, parsley, and wheatgrass to the juicer, and process until juiced. Pour the juice into a glass, and garnish with a sprig of parsley, if desired.

Calories	150	Calcium	123 mg
Calories from fat	7	Iron	3 mg
Total fat	0.79 g	Folic acid	105 mcg
Carbohydrates	33 g	Vitamin K	418 mcg
Protein	5 g	Magnesium	59 mg
Fiber	10 g	Potassium	1233 mg

Wheatgrass— The Champion of Breakfasts

This medley of wheatgrass and other healthful ingredients is definitely a gold medal winner.

2 SERVINGS

4 carrots, cut into 2- to 3-inch lengths

1 apple, cut into eighths

2 celery stalks, cut into 2- to 3-inch lengths

½ small sweet potato, halved

8 sprigs of parsley

1 to 2 ounces wheatgrass

Alternate adding the carrots, apple, celery, sweet potato, parsley, and wheatgrass to the juicer, and process until juiced. Pour the juice into two glasses, and garnish each with a sprig of parsley, if desired.

Calories	150	Calcium	72 mg
Calories from fat	6	Iron	2 mg
Total fat	0.71 g	Folic acid	44 mcg
Carbohydrates	35 g	Vitamin K	212 mcg
Protein	3 g	Magnesium	35 mg
Fiber	8 g	Potassium	748 mg

CHAPTER 6

Excitement in a Glass

Exotic Juices in Your Own Kitchen

As delicious as juices are made from a single fruit or vegetable, you will find that many combinations of the two, such as carrot and apple or fennel and apple, are exceptionally appealing in taste. This chapter presents more than sixty recipes, including such exotic creations as Mean Nectarine, Mr. Tangerine Man, and Drink Your Spinach. You will find these delectably refreshing, but keep in mind that substitutions are always in order. For example, if cabbage is something you'd rather see nestled next to a portion of corned beef than as a juice ingredient, then substitute spinach, kale, or lettuce, or just eliminate it. If you adore carrots more than red peppers, add an extra carrot and eliminate the red pepper. The key to creating these exciting juices is to unleash your creative spirit and have a lot of fun.

Adam's Apple

This juice is dedicated to my son Adam, whose love for juices is second only to his infatuation with automobiles.

1 SERVING

½ cup packed spinach

1 apple, cut into eighths

4 asparagus spears, halved

2 carrots, cut into 2- to 3-inch lengths

2 celery stalks, cut into 2- to 3-inch lengths

Alternate adding the spinach, apple, asparagus, carrots, and celery to the juicer, and process until juiced. Pour the juice into a glass, and garnish the rim with a Cucumber Wheel (page 211), if desired.

Calories	174	Calcium	109 mg
Calories from fat	10	Iron	2 mg
Total fat	1 g	Folic acid	157 mcg
Carbohydrates	42 g	Vitamin K	301 mcg
Protein	4 g	Magnesium	61 mg
Fiber	11 g	Potassium	1112 mg

The Age of Asparagus

Let your hair down while you savor this juice with the distinctive flavor of asparagus.

1 SERVING

6 asparagus spears, halved

4 carrots, cut into 2- to 3-inch lengths

2 celery stalks, cut into 2- to 3-inch lengths

Alternate adding the asparagus, carrots, and celery to the juicer, and process until juiced. Pour the juice into a glass, and garnish the rim with a Cucumber Wheel (page 211), if desired.

Calories	159	Calcium	130 mg
Calories from fat	8	Iron	3 mg
Total fat	0.85 g	Folic acid	186 mcg
Carbohydrates	36 g	Vitamin K	456 mcg
Protein	6 g	Magnesium	69 mg
Fiber	12 g	Potassium	1422 mg

Aladda Colada

You've got pineapple, coconut, and banana. Mix them all together, yada yada yada, and voilà—Aladda Colada!

2 SERVINGS

3 cups peeled and sliced banana

1 ½ cups Yada Yada Yada Piña Colada (page 178)

Place the banana in a blender and mix until pureed. Add the Yada Yada Yada Piña Colada; mix until smooth. Pour the juice into two glasses, and garnish each with a Pineapple, Orange, and Cherry Blossom (page 217), if desired.

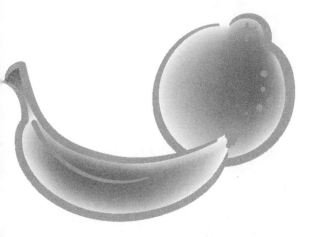

Calories	423	Calcium	28 mg
Calories from fat	146	Iron	2 mg
Total fat	16 g	Beta Carotene	123 mcg
Carbohydrates	75 g	Folic acid	68 mcg
Protein	4 g	Magnesium	97 mg
Fiber	11 g	Potassium	1190 mg

An Apple a Day

This juice is exactly what the doctor ordered. And what's more, it tastes good, too.

1 SERVING

1 apple, cut into eighths

1 celery stalk, cut into 2- to 3-inch lengths

1 small lime, peeled and halved

Alternate adding the apple, celery, and lime to the juicer, and process until juiced. Pour the juice into a glass and garnish the rim with a slice of lime, if desired.

Calories	108	Calcium	48 mg
Calories from fat	6	Iron	0.81 mg
Total fat	0.69 g	Beta Carotene	63 mcg
Carbohydrates	30 g	Vitamin C	30 mg
Protein	1 g	Folic acid	21 mcg
Fiber	6 g	Potassium	342 mg

Apple in Pear-is

The golden color of this pleasingly sweet juice is surely an "Eiffel." Your family and friends will not have "de Gaulle" to do anything but rave about this creation.

1 SERVING

1 pear, cut into eighths

1 apple, cut into eighths

¼ cup sparkling apple cider

Alternate adding the pear and apple to the juicer, and process until juiced. Pour the juice into a glass; add the cider. Mix well. Garnish the rim of the glass with a Lime Wheel (page 211), if desired.

Calories	206	Calcium	32 mg
Calories from fat	11	Iron	0.87 mg
Total fat	1 g	Beta Carotene	48 mcg
Carbohydrates	53 g	Folic acid	16 mcg
Protein	0.94 g	Magnesium	19 mg
Fiber	8 g	Potassium	434 mg

Apples and Oranges

Why bother comparing apples and oranges, when they taste so great together?

1 SERVING

2 oranges, peeled and segmented

1 apple, cut into eighths

½ cup cranberries

½ cup sparkling apple cider

½ tablespoon superfine sugar, or to taste

Alternate adding the oranges, apple, and cranberries to the juicer, and process until juiced. Pour the juice into a glass, and add the cider and sugar. Mix well. Garnish the rim of the glass with an Orange Wheel (page 211), if desired.

Calories	305	Calcium	126 mg
Calories from fat	9	Iron	1 mg
Total fat	1 g	Beta Carotene	145 mcg
Carbohydrates	78 g	Vitamin C	155 mg
Protein	3 g	Folic acid	84 mcg
Fiber	12 g	Potassium	802 mg

The Beet Goes On

This tangy juice is definitely something to sing about.

1 SERVING

½ beet with top, halved

½ yam, halved

4 carrots, cut into 2- to 3-inch lengths

1 clove garlic

1 slice ginger, peeled and cut ¼- to ½-inch thick

Alternate adding the beet, yam, carrots, garlic, and ginger to the juicer, and process until juiced. Pour the juice into a glass, and garnish with a sprig of parsley, if desired.

Calories	294	Calcium	183 mg
Calories from fat	8	Iron	4 mg
Total fat	0.88 g	Beta Carotene	40547 mcg
Carbohydrates	70 g	Folic acid	120 mcg
Protein	7 g	Vitamin K	419 mcg
Fiber	17 g	Potassium	2139 mg

Berry the Hatchet

Let bygones be bygones and just enjoy this wonderful berry drink.

1 SERVING

I cup cranberries

I cup grapes

I cup raspberries

Alternate adding the cranberries, grapes, and raspberries to the juicer, and process until juiced. Pour the juice into a glass and garnish with a Fruit Skewer (page 212), if desired.

To make a spritzer, add 2 tablespoons sparkling apple cider to the juice and mix.

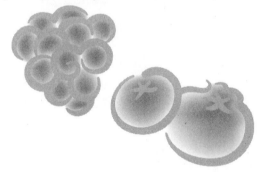

Calories	220	Calcium	51 mg
Calories from fat	16	Iron	I mg
Total fat	2 g	Beta Carotene	142 mcg
Carbohydrates	55 g	Vitamin C	61 mg
Protein	3 g	Folic acid	40 mcg
Fiber	14 g	Potassium	550 mg

The Big Apple

You'll be humming "New York, New York" after one taste of this zesty juice.

1 SERVING

2 apples, cut into eighths

1 orange, peeled and segmented

½ lemon, peeled and halved

Alternate adding the apples, orange, and lemon to the juicer, and process until juiced. Pour the juice into a glass, and garnish the rim with a Lemon Wheel (page 211), if desired.

To make a spritzer, add ¼ cup sparkling mineral water to the juice and mix.

Calories	233	Calcium	79 mg
Calories from fat	11	Iron	0.80 mg
Total fat	1 g	Beta Carotene	113 mcg
Carbohydrates	60 g	Vitamin C	101 mg
Protein	2 g	Folic acid	51 mcg
Fiber	11 g	Potassium	595 mg

Carrot and the Schtick

There is nothing funny about this drink—it simply tastes great.

1 SERVING

3 carrots, cut into 2- to 3-inch lengths

1 apple, cut into eighths

1 orange, peeled and segmented

Alternate adding the carrots, apple, and orange to the juicer, and process until juiced. Pour the juice into a glass, and garnish the rim with a slice of orange, if desired.

Calories	236	Calcium	120 mg
Calories from fat	10	Iron	1 mg
Total fat	1 g	Beta Carotene	29609 mcg
Carbohydrates	58 g	Vitamin C	98 mg
Protein	4 g	Vitamin K	321 mcg
Fiber	13 g	Potassium	1093 mg

Carrotjuice.com

Feeling worn out from surfing the Web? Try a glass of this amazing juice, and then read the following message on the tool bar across the top of your screen: "Now that you're back Home, *this book is certain to become your* Favorite *way in* Print *to* Refresh *yourself."*

1 SERVING

3 carrots, cut into 2- to 3-inch lengths

1 celery stalk, cut into 2- to 3-inch lengths

¼ red bell pepper, halved

2 plum tomatoes, halved

½ cucumber, cut into cubes or spears

1 small lime, peeled and halved

Alternate adding half the carrots, celery, and red pepper to the juicer, then the tomatoes, cucumber, and lime, followed by the remaining ingredients; process until juiced. Pour the juice into a glass, and garnish with a Scallion Flower (page 218), if desired.

Calories	173	Calcium	126 mg
Calories from fat	11	Iron	3 mg
Total fat	1 g	Beta Carotene	31123 mcg
Carbohydrates	42 g	Vitamin C	131 mg
Protein	5 g	Vitamin K	326 mcg
Fiber	12 g	Potassium	1425 mg

Citrus Celebrity

A touch of pineapple added to the lemon, lime, and orange flavors in this juice elevates it to star quality.

2 SERVINGS

1 lemon, peeled and quartered

1 orange, peeled and segmented

1 ½ cups cubed pineapple

½ cup lemon-lime soda

2 teaspoons superfine sugar, or to taste

Alternate adding the lemon, orange, and pineapple to the juicer, and process until juiced. Transfer the juice to a pitcher; add the soda and sugar. Mix well. Pour the juice into two glasses and garnish each with a Lemon and Cranberry Twist (page 213), if desired.

Calories	137	Calcium	43 mg
Calories from fat	6	Iron	0.72 mg
Total fat	0.67 g	Vitamin C	68 mg
Carbohydrates	35 g	Folic acid	35 mcg
Protein	1 g	Magnesium	26 mg
Fiber	4 g	Potassium	291 mg

Cold Carrot Fusion

Don't let anybody tell you that cold fusion is impossible. This invigorating combination of fruits and vegetables proves that it is alive and well in your own kitchen.

1 SERVING

2 carrots, cut into 2- to 3-inch lengths

1 celery stalk, cut into 2- to 3-inch lengths

1 apple, cut into eighths

½ cup cubed pineapple

Alternate adding half the carrots, celery, and apple to the juicer, then the pineapple, followed by the remaining ingredients; process until juiced. Pour the juice into a glass, and garnish with a Lemon and Cranberry Twist (page 213), if desired.

Calories	188	Calcium	70 mg
Calories from fat	10	Iron	1 mg
Total fat	1 g	Beta Carotene	19755 mcg
Carbohydrates	47 g	Vitamin K	216 mcg
Protein	2 g	Magnesium	440 mg
Fiber	10 g	Potassium	826 mg

Cool Hand Cuke

This juice will make you tough enough to handle any challenge.

1 SERVING

3 carrots, cut into 2- to 3-inch lengths

2 celery stalks, cut into 2- to 3-inch lengths

½ cucumber, cut into cubes or spears

4 sprigs parsley

½ small beet with top, halved

Alternate adding the carrots, celery, cucumber, parsley, and beet to the juicer, and process until juiced. Pour the juice into a glass, and garnish the rim with a Cucumber Wheel (page 211), if desired.

Calories	150	Calcium	162 mg
Calories from fat	8	Iron	3 mg
Total fat	0.84 g	Beta Carotene	31082 mcg
Carbohydrates	34 g	Folic acid	128 mcg
Protein	5 g	Vitamin K	314 mcg
Fiber	12 g	Potassium	1474 mg

Cranberry and Raspberry Fizz

This is one fizzy drink you will absolutely adore. The sparkling apple cider adds sweetness and that essential fizz to this terrific combination of cranberries and raspberries.

1 SERVING

1 cup cranberries

1 cup raspberries

½ cup sparkling apple cider

½ tablespoon superfine sugar, or to taste

½ cup crushed ice

Alternate adding the cranberries and raspberries to the juicer, and process until juiced. Transfer the juice to a blender (or covered shaker); add the cider, sugar, and ice, and mix for 30 seconds or until well blended. Pour the juice into a glass, and garnish with Berries on a Skewer (page 210), if desired.

Calories	184	Calcium	48 mg
Calories from fat	9	Iron	1 mg
Total fat	0.99 g	Beta Carotene	76 mcg
Carbohydrates	46 g	Vitamin C	45 mg
Protein	2 g	Folic acid	34 mcg
Fiber	12 g	Potassium	390 mg

Cran Prix

This high-performance juice will get you off to a winning start each morning!

1 SERVING

1 orange, peeled and segmented

¾ cup cranberries

½ grapefruit, peeled and segmented

¼ cup lemon-lime soda

½ to 1 tablespoon superfine sugar, or to taste

Alternate adding the orange, cranberries, and grapefruit to the juicer, and process until juiced. Pour the juice into a glass; add the soda and sugar. Mix well. Garnish with a Lemon and Cranberry Twist (page 213), if desired.

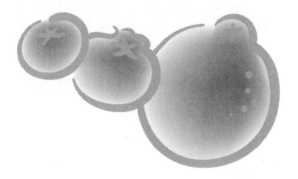

Calories	184	Calcium	73 mg
Calories from fat	4	Iron	0.39 mg
Total fat	0.42 g	Beta Carotene	79 mcg
Carbohydrates	47 g	Vitamin C	119 mg
Protein	2 g	Folic acid	53 mcg
Fiber	7 g	Potassium	463 mg

Cucumber Cooler

Cool your heels with this unusual combination of cucumber and fruit.

1 SERVING

½ cucumber, cut into cubes or spears

1 apple, cut into eighths

1 cup grapes

6 strawberries

Alternate adding the cucumber, apple, grapes, and strawberries to the juicer, and process until juiced. Pour the juice into a glass, and garnish the rim with a strawberry, if desired.

Calories	236	Calcium	58 mg
Calories from fat	17	Iron	1 mg
Total fat	2 g	Beta Carotene	296 mcg
Carbohydrates	59 g	Vitamin C	74 mg
Protein	3 g	Folic acid	42 mcg
Fiber	8 g	Potassium	791 mg

Don't spare the Asparagus

Asparagus can be so good when made into a juice with a touch of other vegetables such as carrot and celery. Enjoy it any time of the day.

1 SERVING

6 asparagus spears, halved

4 carrots, cut into 2- to 3-inch lengths

2 celery stalks, cut into 2- to 3-inch lengths

Alternate adding the asparagus, carrots, and celery to the juicer, and process until juiced. Pour the juice into a glass, and garnish with a celery stalk with leaves, if desired.

Calories	159	Calcium	130 mg
Calories from fat	8	Iron	3 mg
Total fat	0.85 g	Beta Carotene	39764 mcg
Carbohydrates	36 g	Folic acid	186 mcg
Protein	6 g	Vitamin K	456 mcg
Fiber	12 g	Potassium	14220 mg

Drink Your Spinach!

After tasting this flavorful creation, no one will have to remind you to eat your spinach.

1 SERVING

½ cup packed spinach

3 asparagus spears, halved

2 carrots, cut into 2- to 3-inch lengths

1 celery stalk, cut into 2- to 3-inch lengths

Alternate adding the spinach, asparagus, carrots, and celery to the juicer, and process until juiced. Pour the juice into a glass and garnish with a Scallion Flower (page 218), if desired.

Calories	83	Calcium	80 mg
Calories from fat	4	Iron	2 mg
Total fat	0.48 g	Beta Carotene	20480 mcg
Carbohydrates	19 g	Folic acid	122 mcg
Protein	3 g	Vitamin K	288 mcg
Fiber	6 g	Potassium	795 mg

Farmer's Market

This delectable juice contains just a sampling of the wonderful variety of fresh vegetables and fruits you can find at a farmer's market.

1 SERVING

6 carrots, cut into 2- to 3-inch lengths

1 apple, cut into eighths

1 small beet with top, halved

½ sweet potato, cut into cubes

Alternate adding the carrots, apple, beet, and sweet potato to the juicer, and process until juiced. Pour the juice into a glass, and garnish the rim with a slice of lime, if desired.

Calories	377	Calcium	192 mg
Calories from fat	15	Iron	5 mg
Total fat	2 g	Beta Carotene	68090 mcg
Carbohydrates	90 g	Folic acid	167 mcg
Protein	8 g	Vitamin K	636 mcg
Fiber	22 g	Potassium	2128 mg

First Mango on the Moon

Combining this tasty fruit with pineapple and lime is one small step for mango and one giant leap for juicing!

1 SERVING

1 mango, peeled, pitted, and cut into cubes

1 cup cubed pineapple

1 lime, peeled and halved

2 tablespoons sparkling mineral water

1 tablespoon superfine sugar, or to taste

½ cup crushed ice

Alternate adding the mango, pineapple, and lime to the juicer, and process until juiced. Transfer the juice to a blender (or covered shaker); add the water, sugar, and ice, and mix for 30 seconds or until well blended. Pour the juice into a glass, and garnish with a Fruit Skewer (page 212), if desired.

Calories	279	Calcium	54 mg
Calories from fat	12	Iron	1 mg
Total fat	1 g	Beta Carotene	4853 mcg
Carbohydrates	79 g	Vitamin C	101 mg
Protein	2 g	Folic acid	51 mcg
Fiber	7 g	Potassium	567 mg

Follow Your Passion

The sweet-tart flavor of the passion fruit makes it a perfect blend with the sweeter fruits found in this recipe.

1 SERVING

2 passion fruit, halved

1 cup grapes

½ cup cubed pineapple

4 strawberries

Alternate adding the passion fruit, grapes, pineapple, and strawberries to the juicer, and process until juiced. Pour the juice into a glass, and garnish with a Pineapple, Orange, and Cherry Blossom (page 217), if desired.

To make a spritzer, add ¼ cup sparkling mineral water to the juice and blend.

Calories	201	Calcium	34 mg
Calories from fat	15	Iron	1 mg
Total fat	2 g	Beta Carotene	121 mcg
Carbohydrates	50 g	Vitamin C	67 mg
Protein	2 g	Magnesium	36 mg
Fiber	7 g	Potassium	589 mg

The Grape Divide

You'll discover a mountain of flavors from the range of fruits included in this nicely balanced drink.

1 SERVING

1 apple, cut into eighths

1 cup grapes

1 orange, peeled and segmented

Add half the apple to the juicer, then the grapes and orange, followed by the remaining apple; process until juiced. Pour the juice into a glass, and garnish the rim with a slice of orange, if desired.

Calories	257	Calcium	80 mg
Calories from fat	14	Iron	0.80 mg
Total fat	2 g	Beta Carotene	146 mcg
Carbohydrates	65 g	Vitamin C	95 mg
Protein	3 g	Folic acid	50 mcg
Fiber	8 g	Potassium	692 mg

The Grape Gatsby

The wealth of flavors in this juice will be the talk of the town!

1 SERVING

2 carrots, cut into 2- to 3-inch lengths

½ apple, quartered

1 cup grapes

½ orange, peeled and segmented

Alternate adding half the carrots and apple to the juicer, then the grapes and orange, followed by the remaining half of ingredients; process until juiced. Pour the juice into a glass, and garnish the rim with an Orange Wheel (page 211), if desired.

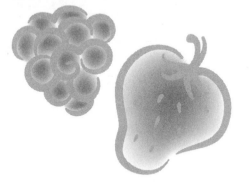

Calories	247	Calcium	88 mg
Calories from fat	14	Iron	1 mg
Total fat	2 g	Beta Carotene	19792 mcg
Carbohydrates	61 g	Vitamin C	69 mg
Protein	3 g	Vitamin K	213 mcg
Fiber	9 g	Potassium	959 mg

Grape, Orange, and Kiwi Collider

When these fruits collide, they produce a smashing juice treat.

1 SERVING

1 cup grapes

1 orange, peeled and segmented

3 kiwis, halved

½ tablespoon superfine sugar, or to taste

½ cup crushed ice

Alternate adding the grapes, orange, and kiwis to the juicer, and process until juiced. Transfer the juice to a blender (or covered shaker); add the sugar and ice, and mix for 30 seconds or until well blended. Pour the juice into a glass, and garnish the rim with a slice of kiwi, if desired.

Calories	355	Calcium	158 mg
Calories from fat	23	Iron	2 mg
Total fat	3 g	Beta Carotene	243 mcg
Carbohydrates	83 g	Vitamin C	306 mg
Protein	5 g	Magnesium	64 mg
Fiber	13 g	Potassium	1274 mg

The Grapefruit Dead

Throw on your favorite tie-dyed shirt and rocket back to the sixties with this groovy, berry-spiked grapefruit creation.

1 SERVING

1 small grapefruit, peeled and segmented

1 cup cranberries

6 strawberries

¼ cup sparkling apple cider

1 tablespoon superfine sugar, or to taste

Alternate adding the grapefruit, cranberries, and strawberries to the juicer, and process until juiced. Pour the juice into a glass, and add the cider and sugar. Mix well. Garnish the rim of the glass with a strawberry, if desired.

Calories	221	Calcium	49 mg
Calories from fat	7	Iron	0.82 mg
Total fat	0.75 g	Vitamin C	133 mg
Carbohydrates	56 g	Folic acid	38 mcg
Protein	2 g	Magnesium	35 mg
Fiber	8 g	Potassium	604 mg

Green with Envy

Your friends will covet the spring in your step after you've indulged in this healthful combination of apple and four vegetables.

1 SERVING

4 celery stalks, cut into 2- to 3-inch lengths

½ cucumber, cut into cubes or spears

½ cup packed spinach

1 apple, cut into eighths

⅛ head (about 3 ounces) cabbage, halved

Alternate adding the celery, cucumber, spinach, apple, and cabbage to the juicer, and process until juiced. Pour the juice into a glass, and garnish the rim with a Cucumber Wheel (page 211), if desired.

Calories	158	Calcium	163 mg
Calories from fat	11	Iron	2 mg
Total fat	1 g	Beta Carotene	1029 mcg
Carbohydrates	38 g	Folic acid	146 mcg
Protein	5 g	Magnesium	70 mg
Fiber	11 g	Potassium	1198 mg

Grin and Carrot

This salad in a glass will definitely put a smile on your face.

1 SERVING

4 carrots, cut into 2- to 3-inch lengths

1 celery stalk, cut into 2- to 3-inch lengths

1 cup red leaf lettuce

8 sprigs parsley

Alternate adding the carrots, celery, lettuce, and parsley to the juicer, and process until juiced. Pour the juice into a glass, and garnish with a celery stalk with leaves, if desired.

Calories	140	Calcium	123 mg
Calories from fat	7	Iron	2 mg
Total fat	0.79 g	Beta Carotene	39979 mcg
Carbohydrates	32 g	Folic acid	105 mcg
Protein	4 g	Vitamin K	418 mcg
Fiber	10 g	Potassium	1233 mg

Heard It Through the Grapefruit

Pucker up for this delightfully tangy juice.

1 SERVING

1 orange, peeled and segmented

1 grapefruit, peeled and segmented

1 slice lime, peeled and cut ½-inch thick

¼ cup lemon-lime soda

½ teaspoon superfine sugar, or to taste

½ teaspoon grenadine (optional)

Alternate adding the orange, grapefruit, and lime to the juicer, and process until juiced. Pour the juice into a glass, and add the soda, sugar, and optional grenadine. Mix well. Garnish the rim of the glass with a slice of lime, if desired.

Calories	175	Calcium	85 mg
Calories from fat	4	Iron	0.37 mg
Total fat	0.41 g	Vitamin C	151 mg
Carbohydrates	45 g	Folic acid	64 mcg
Protein	3 g	Magnesium	35 mg
Fiber	6 g	Potassium	596 mg

Hic-Kiwi Dic-Kiwi Dock

You don't have to wait for the clock to strike one to enjoy this sparkling tropical drink.

1 SERVING

12 strawberries

1 cup cubed pineapple

1 kiwi, halved

½ cup crushed ice

2 tablespoons sparkling apple cider (optional)

Alternate adding the strawberries, pineapple, and kiwi to the juicer, and process until juiced. Transfer the juice to a blender (or covered shaker); add the ice and optional cider, and mix for 30 seconds or until well blended. Pour the juice into a glass, and garnish the rim with a strawberry, if desired.

Calories	184	Calcium	62 mg
Calories from fat	16	Iron	2 mg
Total fat	2 g	Beta Carotene	83 mcg
Carbohydrates	43 g	Vitamin C	179 mg
Protein	2 g	Magnesium	51 mg
Fiber	8 g	Potassium	695 mg

The Holy Kale

You won't have to endure a long quest to find this delicious juice—a few spins of the juicer and you can enjoy it any "knight."

1 SERVING

3 carrots, cut into 2- to 3-inch lengths

2 celery stalks, cut into 2- to 3-inch lengths

¼ beet with top

2 kale leaves

Alternate adding the carrots, celery, beet, and kale to the juicer, and process until juiced. Pour the juice into a glass, and garnish with a celery stalk with leaves, if desired.

Calories	144	Calcium	248 mg
Calories from fat	8	Iron	4 mg
Total fat	0.92 g	Beta Carotene	31819 mcg
Carbohydrates	33 g	Vitamin K	777 mcg
Protein	5 g	Magnesium	119 mg
Fiber	11 g	Potassium	1424 mg

I Don't Carrot All

Forget your problems with this unique fruit and vegetable combination!

1 SERVING

4 carrots, cut into 2- to 3-inch lengths

1 cup cubed pineapple

¾ cup sliced banana

1 teaspoon superfine sugar, or to taste

⅛ teaspoon cinnamon

Alternate adding half the carrots to the juicer, then the pineapple, followed by the remaining carrots; process until juiced. Place the banana in a blender, and mix until pureed. Add the juice, sugar, and cinnamon; mix for 30 seconds or until well blended. Pour the juice into a glass, and garnish with a Pineapple, Banana, and Cherry Charmer (page 216), if desired.

Calories	320	Calcium	99 mg
Calories from fat	16	Iron	2 mg
Total fat	2 g	Beta Carotene	39445 mcg
Carbohydrates	79 g	Vitamin K	419 mcg
Protein	5 g	Magnesium	98 mg
Fiber	13 g	Potassium	1552 mg

Island Breeze

The sweetness of orange and pineapple in this juice is as fresh as a tropical breeze all year long.

1 SERVING

1 ½ cups cubed pineapple

1 orange, peeled and segmented

¼ cup sparkling mineral water

Alternate adding the pineapple and orange to the juicer, and process until juiced. Pour the juice into a glass, and add the sparkling water. Mix well. Garnish with a Pineapple, Banana and Cherry Charmer (page 216), if desired.

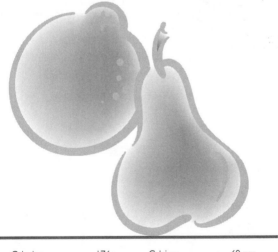

Calories	176	Calcium	69 mg
Calories from fat	10	Iron	0.99 mg
Total fat	1 g	Vitamin C	106 mg
Carbohydrates	44 g	Folic acid	64 mcg
Protein	2 g	Magnesium	46 mg
Fiber	6 g	Potassium	500 mg

Jumping Ginger, Carrot, and Apple

This juice really gets a flavor jolt when ginger is added to the other ingredients.

1 SERVING

4 carrots, cut into 2- to 3-inch lengths

1 apple, cut into eighths

1 slice ginger, peeled and cut ¼- to ½-inch thick

Alternate adding the carrots, apple, and ginger to the juicer, and process until juiced. Pour the juice into a glass, and garnish the rim with a Lemon Wheel (page 211), if desired.

Calories	207	Calcium	88 mg
Calories from fat	10	Iron	2 mg
Total fat	1 g	Beta Carotene	39401 mcg
Carbohydrates	51 g	Vitamin K	425 mcg
Protein	3 g	Magnesium	51 mg
Fiber	12 g	Potassium	1099 mg

Kiwi Witness

You be the judge. This combination of sweet kiwi and strawberries, with just a taste of tart cranberry, is so enjoyable it should be against the law.

1 SERVING

2 kiwi, halved

1 cup cranberries

8 strawberries

Alternate adding the kiwis, cranberries, and strawberries to the juicer, and process until juiced. Pour the juice into a glass, and garnish the rim with a strawberry, if desired.

Calories	179	Calcium	79 mg
Calories from fat	14	Iron	1 mg
Total fat	2 g	Beta Carotene	127 mcg
Carbohydrates	40 g	Vitamin C	213 mg
Protein	2 g	Magnesium	42 mg
Fiber	11 g	Potassium	721 mg

Liquid Lifesaver

This sprightly juice contains many of the flavors found in the popular Lifesaver candies.

2 SERVINGS

I cup grapes

I cup cranberries

I kiwi, halved

I apple, cut into eighths

½ lemon, peeled and halved

I cup cubed pineapple

Alternate adding the grapes, cranberries, kiwi, apple, lemon, and pineapple to the juicer, and process until juiced. Pour into two glasses, and garnish each with a Lemon and Cranberry Twist (page 213), if desired.

Calories	189	Calcium	41 mg
Calories from fat	13	Iron	0.99 mg
Total fat	1 g	Vitamin C	75 mg
Carbohydrates	47 g	Folic acid	16 mcg
Protein	2 g	Magnesium	29 mg
Fiber	7 g	Potassium	492 mg

Mango Fandango

This wonderfully sweet and fizzy glassful could pass for a cousin of Asti Spumante.

1 SERVING

1 mango, peeled, pitted, and cut into cubes

1 banana, peeled and cubed

¼ cup sparkling apple cider

½ tablespoon superfine sugar, or to taste

½ cup crushed ice

Add the mango to the juicer and process until juiced. Place the banana in a blender, and mix until pureed. Add the juice, cider, sugar, and ice to the blender and process for 30 seconds or until well blended. Pour the juice into a glass, and garnish with a Pineapple, Banana, and Cherry Charmer (page 216), if desired.

Calories	294	Calcium	32 mg
Calories from fat	11	Iron	0.85 mg
Total fat	1 g	Beta Carotene	4888 mcg
Carbohydrates	76 g	Vitamin C	69 mg
Protein	2 g	Magnesium	55 mg
Fiber	7 g	Potassium	858 mg

Mango of La Mancha

To enjoy this appealing combination, just pop both fruits into the juicer and live the impossible dream.

1 SERVING

2 oranges, peeled and segmented

1 mango, peeled, pitted, and cubed

Alternate adding the oranges and mango to the juicer, and process until juiced. Pour the juice into a glass, and garnish the rim with a slice of orange, if desired.

To make a spritzer, add 2 tablespoons sparkling apple cider to the juice and mix.

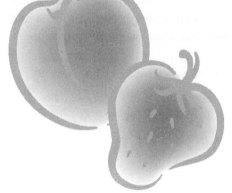

Calories	258	Calcium	126 mg
Calories from fat	8	Iron	0.53 mg
Total fat	0.87 g	Beta Carotene	4934 mcg
Carbohydrates	66 g	Vitamin C	197 mg
Protein	4 g	Folic acid	108 mcg
Fiber	10 g	Potassium	797 mg

Mean Nectarine

A choice way to get your vitamin C in a most excellent juice.

1 SERVING

1 nectarine, pitted and quartered

½ orange, peeled and segmented

½ grapefruit, peeled and segmented

2 tablespoons mineral water

½ tablespoon superfine sugar, or to taste

Alternate adding the nectarine, orange, and grapefruit to the juicer, and process until juiced. Pour the juice into a glass, and add the water and sugar. Mix well. Garnish the rim of the glass with an Orange and Blueberry Twist (page 213), if desired.

Calories	161	Calcium	47 mg
Calories from fat	7	Iron	0.34 mg
Total fat	0.82 g	Beta Carotene	532 mcg
Carbohydrates	40 g	Vitamin C	81 mg
Protein	3 g	Magnesium	28 mg
Fiber	5 g	Potassium	582 mg

Mr. Tangerine Man

In the jingle jangle morning, this unusual and delightful combination of tangerine and pomegranate will have you singing for more.

1 SERVING

1 pomegranate, peeled, seeded, and cut into eighths (reserve seeds, discard skin)

1 tangerine, peeled, seeded, and segmented

¼ cup sparkling apple cider

2 teaspoons superfine sugar, or to taste

Alternate adding the pomegranate seeds and tangerine to the juicer, and process until juiced. Transfer the juice to a blender (or covered shaker); add the cider and sugar, and mix for 30 seconds or until well blended. Pour the juice into a glass, and garnish with a Fruit Skewer (page 212), if desired.

Calories	201	Calcium	20 mg
Calories from fat	6	Iron	0.76 mg
Total fat	0.68 g	Beta Carotene	464 mcg
Carbohydrates	51 g	Vitamin C	36 mg
Protein	2 g	Folic acid	26 mcg
Fiber	3 g	Potassium	598 mg

Peaches in Seattle

Searching for just the right juice to make your life happier? This slightly tangy creation is the juice that you are destined to fall in love with.

1 SERVING

2 peaches, pitted and quartered

1 cup grapes

¼ cup sparkling apple cider

Alternate adding the peaches and grapes to the juicer, and process until juiced. Pour the juice into a glass and add the cider. Mix well. Garnish the rim of the glass with a slice of peach, if desired.

Calories	225	Calcium	31 mg
Calories from fat	11	Iron	0.84 mg
Total fat	1 g	Beta Carotene	588 mcg
Carbohydrates	57 g	Vitamin C	31 mg
Protein	2 g	Magnesium	25 mg
Fiber	6 g	Potassium	750 mg

The Pear Essentials

What more do you need to make a delicious fruit drink than a pear and a few other tasty ingredients?

1 SERVING

1 pear, cut into eighths

1 peach, pitted and quartered

1 cup cranberries

1 cup cubed pineapple

Alternate adding the pear, peach, cranberries, and pineapple to the juicer, and process until juiced. Pour the juice into a glass, and garnish with a Lemon and Cranberry Twist (page 213), if desired.

Calories	263	Calcium	41 mg
Calories from fat	14	Iron	1 mg
Total fat	2 g	Beta Carotene	326 mcg
Carbohydrates	67 g	Vitamin C	50 mg
Protein	2 g	Magnesium	43 mg
Fiber	12 g	Potassium	643 mg

Planet of the Grapes

You will go absolutely ape over this pleasingly sweet juice sensation.

1 SERVING

1 cup grapes

8 strawberries

½ cup raspberries

1 banana, peeled and cubed

Alternate adding the grapes, strawberries, and raspberries to the juicer, and process until juiced. Place the banana in a blender, and mix until pureed. Add the juice to the blender; mix for 30 seconds or until well blended. Pour the juice into a glass, and garnish the rim with a strawberry, if desired.

To make a sparkling drink, add ½ cup sparkling apple cider to the juice and mix.

Calories	281	Calcium	52 mg
Calories from fat	20	Iron	2 mg
Total fat	2 g	Beta Carotene	162 mcg
Carbohydrates	70 g	Vitamin C	98 mg
Protein	3 g	Magnesium	64 mg
Fiber	11 g	Potassium	1016 mg

Rasmanian Devil Lemonade

This lemonade is one mean drink; but even if you are not from Down Under, you'll keep coming back for more.

1 SERVING

1 cup raspberries

1 kiwi, halved

1 small lemon, peeled and halved

6 tablespoons sparkling mineral water

1 to 2 tablespoons superfine sugar, or to taste

¼ cup crushed ice

Alternate adding the raspberries, kiwi, and lemon to the juicer, and process until juiced. Transfer the juice to a blender (or covered shaker); add the water, sugar, and ice, and mix for 30 seconds (combined) or until well mixed. Pour the juice into a glass, and garnish with Berries on a Skewer (page 210), if desired.

Calories	177	Calcium	72 mg
Calories from fat	12	Iron	1 mg
Total fat	1 g	Vitamin C	135 mg
Carbohydrates	43 g	Folic acid	38 mcg
Protein	3 g	Magnesium	40 mg
Fiber	13 g	Potassium	514 mg

Razzle Dazzle Raspberry Spritzer

Dazzle your friends and family by serving this sparkling juice.

1 SERVING

1 pint raspberries

1 mango, peeled, pitted, and cut into cubes

2 kiwi, halved

½ cup sparkling mineral water

1½ tablespoons grenadine

½ tablespoon superfine sugar, or to taste

Alternate adding the raspberries, mango, and kiwis to the juicer, and process until juiced. Pour the juice into a glass, and add the water, grenadine, and sugar. Mix well. Garnish with Berries on a Skewer (page 210), if desired.

Calories	463	Calcium	136 mg
Calories from fat	26	Iron	2 mg
Total fat	3 g	Beta Carotene	5011 mcg
Carbohydrates	113 g	Vitamin C	266 mg
Protein	5 g	Magnesium	91 mg
Fiber	26 g	Potassium	1200 mg

Red as a Beet

You will not be embarrassed to say this is one of the best juices you have ever tasted.

1 SERVING

4 carrots, cut into 2- to 3-inch lengths

½ cup packed spinach

½ apple, quartered

⅛ head (3 ounces) of cabbage, halved

½ small beet with top, halved

Alternate adding the carrots, spinach, apple, cabbage, and beet to the juicer, and process until juiced. Pour the juice into a glass, and garnish the rim of the glass with a Cucumber Wheel (page 211), if desired.

Calories	220	Calcium	195 mg
Calories from fat	11	Iron	4 mg
Total fat	1 g	Beta Carotene	41248 mcg
Carbohydrates	52 g	Folic acid	170 mcg
Protein	6 g	Vitamin K	482 mcg
Fiber	16 g	Potassium	1681 mg

The Spinach That Stole Christmas

Why serve eggnog when you can serve this wonderful juice? Garnish with cranberries on a skewer for the ultimate holiday refreshment.

2 SERVINGS

2 cups packed spinach

6 carrots, cut into 2- to 3-inch lengths

6 celery stalks, cut into 2- to 3-inch lengths

8 sprigs of parsley

Alternate adding the spinach, carrots, celery, and parsley to the juicer, and process until juiced. Pour the juice into two glasses, and garnish each with a sprig of parsley, if desired.

Calories	120	Calcium	142 mg
Calories from fat	6	Iron	3 mg
Total fat	0.72 g	Beta Carotene	30944 mcg
Carbohydrates	28 g	Folic acid	128 mcg
Protein	4 g	Vitamin K	433 mcg
Fiber	9 g	Potassium	1232 mg

Stalk Talk

This richly flavored juice proves that celery is not just for swiping through the curry dip.

2 SERVINGS

8 carrots, cut into 2- to 3-inch lengths

4 celery stalks, cut into 2- to 3-inch lengths

1 apple, cut into eighths

Alternate adding the carrots, celery, and apple to the juicer, and process until juiced. Pour the juice into two glasses, and garnish each with a celery stalk with leaves, if desired.

Calories	177	Calcium	114 mg
Calories from fat	8	Iron	2 mg
Total fat	0.91 g	Beta Carotene	39449 mcg
Carbohydrates	43 g	Folic acid	65 mcg
Protein	4 g	Vitamin K	421 mcg
Fiber	12 g	Potassium	1239 mg

Swingin' Strawberry Lemonade

Put on your zoot suit and cut a rug with this cool, bubbly thirst-quencher.

2 SERVINGS

1 pint (2 cups) strawberries

1 lemon, peeled and halved

1 tablespoon superfine sugar, or to taste

½ cup sparkling mineral water

Alternate adding the strawberries and lemon to the juicer, and process until juiced. Transfer the juice to a pitcher, and add the sugar and mineral water. Mix well. Pour the juice into two glasses, and garnish the rim of each with a Fruit Skewer (page 212), if desired.

Calories	76	Calcium	28 mg
Calories from fat	6	Iron	0.72 mg
Total fat	0.62 g	Beta Carotene	29 mcg
Carbohydrates	19 g	Vitamin C	97 mg
Protein	1 g	Folic acid	29 mcg
Fiber	4 g	Potassium	279 mg

Tangerine Teaser

Tease your taste buds with this choice combination of tangerines, pineapple, and grapes.

1 SERVING

2 tangerines, peeled and segmented

1 cup grapes

½ cup cubed pineapple

¼ cup sparkling mineral water

1 tablespoon superfine sugar, or to taste

½ cup crushed ice

Alternate adding the tangerines, grapes, and pineapple to the juicer, and process until juiced. Transfer the juice to a blender (or covered shaker); add the water, sugar, and ice, and mix for 30 seconds or until well blended. Pour the juice into a glass, and garnish with a Lemon and Cranberry Twist (page 213), if desired.

Calories	274	Calcium	42 mg
Calories from fat	14	Iron	0.88 mg
Total fat	2 g	Beta Carotene	1003 mcg
Carbohydrates	69 g	Vitamin C	81 mg
Protein	2 g	Folic acid	49 mcg
Fiber	6 g	Potassium	648 mg

Tomato Tornado

Grab Toto (or your household's equivalent) and take cover! This is one powerfully tasty juice.

2 SERVINGS

6 carrots, cut into 2- to 3-inch lengths

6 celery stalks, cut into 2- to 3-inch lengths

¼ red bell pepper

2 tomatoes, quartered

Alternate adding half the carrots, celery, and red pepper to the juicer, then the tomatoes, followed by the remaining half of the ingredients; process until juiced. Pour the juice into two glasses, and garnish each with a celery stalk with leaves, if desired.

Calories	142	Calcium	114 mg
Calories from fat	9	Iron	3 mg
Total fat	1 g	Beta Carotene	30529 mcg
Carbohydrates	3 g	Folic acid	86 mcg
Protein	4 g	Vitamin K	323 mcg
Fiber	10 g	Potassium	1341 mg

Tomato Touchdown

You'll get a real kick from this juice, especially if you add more than the suggested amount of hot pepper sauce.

1 SERVING

2 carrots, cut into 2- to 3-inch lengths

2 celery stalks, cut into 2- to 3-inch lengths

6 plum tomatoes, halved

⅛ teaspoon (more or less) hot pepper sauce

Scant ⅛ teaspoon (or more) ground coriander

Scant ⅛ teaspoon salt

Scant ⅛ teaspoon (or more) freshly ground pepper

Alternate adding half the carrots and celery to the juicer, then the tomatoes, followed by the remaining carrots and celery; process until juiced. Pour the juice into a glass containing three to four ice cubes. Add the hot pepper sauce, coriander, salt, and pepper and mix well. Garnish the rim of the glass with a Lemon Wheel (page 211), if desired.

Calories	154	Calcium	92 mg
Calories from fat	15	Iron	3 mg
Total fat	2 g	Beta Carotene	21102 mcg
Carbohydrates	35 g	Folic acid	99 mcg
Protein	5 g	Vitamin K	231 mcg
Fiber	10 g	Potassium	1531 mg

Tutti Frutti Fizzle

Your kitchen will rock when you roll these five fruits together with sparkling apple cider for a deliciously sweet juice that tickles the tongue.

2 SERVINGS

1 cup cubed pineapple

1 apple, cut into eighths

1 orange, peeled and segmented

½ cup grapes

½ cup cubed cantaloupe (or favorite melon)

6 tablespoons sparkling apple cider

Alternate adding the pineapple, apple, orange, grapes, and cantaloupe to the juicer, and process until juiced. Transfer the juice to a pitcher, and add the cider. Blend well. Pour the juice into two glasses, and garnish each with Melon Balls on a Skewer (page 214), if desired.

Calories	172	Calcium	48 mg
Calories from fat	9	Iron	0.82 mg
Total fat	1 g	Beta Carotene	833 mcg
Carbohydrates	43 g	Vitamin C	72 mg
Protein	2 g	Folic acid	38 mcg
Fiber	5 g	Potassium	534 mg

(Twenty-) Four-Carrot Gold

Carrot juice is richly delicious on its own, but in this recipe, the addition of other vegetables and spices gives it an extra zing.

1 SERVING

4 carrots, cut into 2- to 3-inch lengths

¼ red bell pepper

½ cucumber, cut into cubes or spears

½ cup spinach

2 cloves garlic

1 small lemon, peeled and halved

Alternate adding the carrots, red bell pepper, cucumber, spinach, garlic, and lemon to the juicer, and process until juiced. Pour the juice into a glass, and garnish with a celery stalk with leaves, if desired.

Calories	181	Calcium	142 mg
Calories from fat	10	Iron	3 mg
Total fat	1 g	Vitamin C	128 mg
Carbohydrates	43 g	Folic acid	102 mcg
Protein	6 g	Vitamin K	483 mcg
Fiber	13 g	Potassium	1387 mg

Vanity Pear

This high-class juice is a novel creation the whole family can enjoy.

1 SERVING

1 pear, cut into eighths

1 mango, peeled, pitted and cut into cubes

6 strawberries

Alternate adding the pear, mango, and strawberries to the juicer, and process until juiced. Pour the juice into a glass, and garnish the rim with a strawberry, if desired.

Calories	254	Calcium	49 mg
Calories from fat	13	Iron	0.96 mg
Total fat	1 g	Vitamin C	105 mg
Carbohydrates	65 g	Folic acid	54 mcg
Protein	2 g	Magnesium	36 mg
Fiber	9 g	Potassium	650 mg

Veggie Blast

There is no better way to describe this zesty combination—dynamite!

2 SERVINGS

8 carrots, cut into 2- to 3-inch lengths

2 celery stalks, cut into 2- to 3-inch lengths

½ beet with top, halved

½ small cucumber, cut into cubes or spears

½ small sweet potato, halved

Alternate adding the carrots, celery, beet, cucumber, and sweet potato to the juicer, and process until juiced. Pour the juice into two glasses, and garnish each with a celery stalk with leaves, if desired.

Calories	186	Calcium	134 mg
Calories from fat	8	Iron	3 mg
Total fat	0.84 g	Folic acid	91 mcg
Carbohydrates	43 g	Vitamin K	418 mcg
Protein	5 g	Magnesium	75 mg
Fiber	12 g	Potassium	1374 mg

Vincent Man-goh

Lend an ear! This mango juice is a genuine work of art.

1 SERVING

2 passion fruit, halved

1 mango, peeled, pitted, and cut into cubes

1 pear, cut into eighths

Alternate adding the passion fruit, mango, and pear to the juicer, and process until juiced. Pour the juice into a glass, and garnish with a Pineapple, Orange, and Cherry Blossom (page 217), if desired.

Calories	267	Calcium	43 mg
Calories from fat	13	Iron	1 mg
Total fat	1 g	Vitamin C	75 mg
Carbohydrates	69 g	Folic acid	46 mcg
Protein	3 g	Magnesium	39 mg
Fiber	11 g	Potassium	656 mg

The Viper V-10

One glance under the hood will confirm that a V-10 is more powerful than a V-8. So start your juice engines and enjoy this healthful cornucopia in a glass.

2 SERVINGS

4 carrots, cut into 2- to 3-inch lengths

1 celery stalk, cut into 2- to 3-inch lengths

½ cup packed spinach

¼ small beet with top, halved

¼ red bell pepper

4 sprigs parsley

2 sprigs watercress

1 clove garlic, peeled

¼ cucumber, cubed

2 plum tomatoes, halved

Alternate adding half the carrots, celery, spinach, beet, red bell pepper, parsley, watercress, and garlic to the juicer, then the cucumber and tomatoes, followed by the remaining half of the ingredients; process until juiced. Pour the juice into two glasses and mix well. Garnish each with a celery stalk with leaves, if desired.

Calories	99	Calcium	93 mg
Calories from fat	6	Iron	2 mg
Total fat	0.66 g	Beta Carotene	21452 mcg
Carbohydrates	23 g	Folic acid	75 mcg
Protein	3 g	Vitamin K	252 mcg
Fiber	7 g	Potassium	929 mg

We Got the Beet!

March to the "beet" of a different drummer. This wonderful vegetable adds a distinctive tangy flavor to this healthful creation.

2 SERVINGS

6 carrots, cut into 2- to 3-inch lengths

2 celery stalks, cut into 2- to 3-inch lengths

1 small beet with top, halved

2 tomatoes, quartered

Alternate adding half the carrots, celery, and beet to the juicer, then the tomatoes, followed by the remaining half of the ingredients; process until juiced. Pour the juice into two glasses, and garnish each with a celery stalk with leaves, if desired.

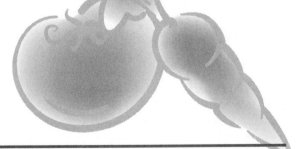

Calories	146	Calcium	106 mg
Calories from fat	9	Iron	3 mg
Total fat	0.95 g	Beta Carotene	30597 mcg
Carbohydrates	34 g	Folic acid	107 mcg
Protein	5 g	Vitamin K	322 mcg
Fiber	10 g	Potassium	1306 mg

Whose Lime Is It Anyway?

No need to improvise with this drink. The combination of lime, mango, and strawberries is already perfect.

1 SERVING

1 mango, peeled, pitted, and cut into cubes

6 strawberries

1 small lime, peeled and halved

½ cup sparkling apple cider

½ tablespoon superfine sugar, or to taste

Alternate adding the mango, strawberries, and lime to the juicer, and process until juiced. Pour the juice into a glass, and add the cider and sugar. Mix well. Garnish the rim of the glass with a strawberry, if desired.

Calories	254	Calcium	61 mg
Calories from fat	10	Iron	1 mg
Total fat	1 g	Beta Carotene	4847 mcg
Carbohydrates	67 g	Vitamin C	119 mg
Protein	2 g	Folic acid	47 mcg
Fiber	7 g	Potassium	646 mg

Would You Carrot to Dance Smoothie

Although you don't often find a recipe for a smoothie in a juicing cookbook, I could not resist adding this one that is made with fresh carrot juice. The carrot juice should be well chilled, and the apple and banana should be placed in the freezer for at least 30 minutes before blending the ingredients into a smoothie.

2 SERVINGS

1 cup carrot juice

½ tablespoon honey

1 cup diced apple

1 cup peeled and sliced banana

½ cup plain nonfat yogurt

¾ cup crushed ice

Place the carrot juice, honey, apple, banana, yogurt, and ice in a blender; mix on low speed until the banana is pureed. Continue mixing, gradually increasing the speed, until the mixture is smooth. Pour into two glasses and garnish each with an Orange, Lemon, and Cherry Combo (page 215), if desired.

Calories	167	Calcium	116 mg
Calories from fat	7	Iron	0.35 mg
Total fat	0.73 g	Beta Carotene	1299 mcg
Carbohydrates	4 g	Folic acid	16 mcg
Protein	4 g	Magnesium	25 mg
Fiber	3 g	Potassium	621 mg

Yada Yada Yada Piña Colada

Did you know that coconuts and pineapples are considered a sign many feel represents the art of endless self-absorbed chatter.

2 SERVINGS

2 cups cubed coconut

3 cups cubed pineapple

To open a fresh coconut, locate the three "eyes" on the small end of the coconut. Using a clean screwdriver, tap the end into each eye with a hammer or mallet. Pour the coconut liquid into a strainer placed over a glass.

Place the coconut on a flat surface, and tap the coconut with a knife about a third of the way down from the small end. Turn the coconut slightly and tap it. Continue this process until you see a fracture. Insert the tip of the knife into the fracture, and pry upward or until the coconut breaks open. Using a spoon or knife, pry the flesh from the shell and remove the brown membrane with a vegetable peeler. Rinse the coconut under cold water and dry.

Calories	397	Calcium	27 mg
Calories from fat	250	Iron	3 mg
Total fat	28 g	Vitamin C	38 mg
Carbohydrates	41 g	Folic acid	46 mcg
Protein	4 g	Magnesium	58 mg
Fiber	10 g	Potassium	548 mg

Add half the coconut to the juicer, then the pineapple, followed by the remaining coconut; process until juiced. Pour the juice into two glasses, and blend well. Garnish each with a Pineapple, Orange, and Cherry Blossom (page 217), if desired.

Yakety Yak Jicama

You won't be able to stop talking about this sensational juice made with jicama.

1 SERVING

1 cup packed spinach

⅔ cup cubed jicama

2 carrots, cut into 2- to 3-inch lengths

1 celery stalk, cut into 2- to 3-inch lengths

Alternate adding the spinach, jicama, carrots, and celery to the juicer, and process until juiced. Pour the juice into a glass, and garnish with a celery stalk with leaves, if desired.

Calories	105	Calcium	94 mg
Calories from fat	5	Iron	2 mg
Total fat	0.51 g	Beta Carotene	20923 mcg
Carbohydrates	24 g	Folic acid	99 mcg
Protein	3 g	Vitamin K	329 mcg
Fiber	10 g	Potassium	867 mg

Yam-borghini

Bellisimo! *This wonderfully sleek creation goes down fast.*

1 SERVING

3 carrots, cut into 2- to 3-inch lengths

2 celery stalks, cut into 2- to 3-inch lengths

1 small yam (or sweet potato), cut into cubes

Alternate adding the carrots, celery, and yam to the juicer, and process until juiced. Pour the juice into a glass, and garnish the rim with a Cucumber Wheel (page 211), if desired.

Calories	387	Calcium	200 mg
Calories from fat	8	Iron	4 mg
Total fat	0.94 g	Beta Carotene	29592 mcg
Carbohydrates	93 g	Folic acid	111 mcg
Protein	8 g	Vitamin K	313 mcg
Fiber	20 g	Potassium	2683 mg

You've Got Kale!

Just strike any key to receive a message telling you that credit for this piquant drink goes to Abe, a good friend of one of my sons. The juice has a real zing to it and is a taste sensation that you won't soon forget.

1 SERVING

4 carrots, cut into 2- to 3-inch lengths

2 kale leaves

1 slice ginger, peeled and cut ¼- to ½-inch thick

1 clove garlic

Alternate adding the carrots, kale, ginger, and garlic to the juicer, and process until juiced. Pour the juice into a glass, and garnish the rim with a Cucumber Wheel (page 211), if desired.

Calories	154	Calcium	200 mg
Calories from fat	8	Iron	3 mg
Total fat	0.92 g	Beta Carotene	40427 mcg
Carbohydrates	35 g	Vitamin C	102 mg
Protein	5 g	Vitamin K	881 mcg
Fiber	10 g	Potassium	1208 mg

CHAPTER 7

Shaken,
but Not Stirred

Juicing Cocktails

M ost cocktails that call for fruit juice are made with the bottled or frozen variety, making the preparation quick and easy. But now that you own a juicer, just imagine how much more authentic it will be to prepare cocktails using fresh juice and, what's more, how much more flavorful they will taste. Just as important, at the same time you are enjoying a pre-dinner cocktail, you will also be reaping the health benefits derived from the nutrients in fresh fruit juices. Of course, if you prefer nonalcoholic drinks, you will be delighted to find that many of the recipes in this chapter can be made without the suggested liquors by substituting with sparkling apple cider instead.

So, whether you prefer your juice with spirits or without, when the spirit moves you, you will find over twenty enticing recipes in this chapter. Just like Agent 007, the inspiration for the title of this chapter, you will discover the rewards of squeezing (fruit, in your case) for pleasure.

Apple Jack

This drink reaches new heights when made with fresh apple juice.

1 SERVING

3 apples, cut into eighths

2 tablespoons Jack Daniels

Place the apples in the juicer, and process until juiced. Transfer the apple juice to a covered shaker, and add the Jack Daniels. Shake until well blended. Place three to four ice cubes in a cocktail glass, and add the Apple Jack. Garnish with a Lemon and Cranberry Twist (page 213), if desired.

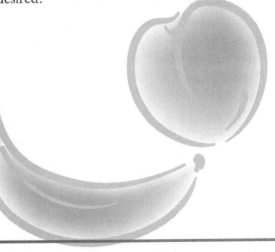

Calories	314	Calcium	29 mg
Calories from fat	13	Iron	0.75 mg
Total fat	1 g	Beta Carotene	84 mcg
Carbohydrates	63 g	Vitamin C	24 mg
Protein	0.79 g	Magnesium	21 mg
Fiber	11 g	Potassium	477 mg

Clementine Tequila Sunrise

Oh, my darlin'! Better than singing about Clementine, enjoy this delectable drink made with the juice from mandarins instead of an ordinary orange.

1 SERVING

2 (or more) clementines, peeled and segmented

3 tablespoons tequila

2 tablespoons grenadine

Place the clementines in the juicer, and process until juiced; you want at least ½ cup juice. Place three ice cubes in a highball glass, and add the tequila. Slowly pour the clementine juice over the tequila, and then the grenadine syrup. Garnish the rim of the glass with an Orange Wheel (page 211), if desired.

Calories	277	Calcium	26 mg
Calories from fat	3	Iron	0.25 mg
Total fat	0.34 g	Beta Carotene	927 mcg
Carbohydrates	47 g	Vitamin C	53 mg
Protein	1 g	Folic acid	35 mcg
Fiber	4 g	Potassium	277 mg

'57 Chevy

What a cool way to bring back the good old days of the fifties.

1 SERVING

2½ cups cubed pineapple

2 tablespoons vodka

2 tablespoons Grand Marnier

2 tablespoons Southern Comfort

Place the pineapple in the juicer, and process until juiced. Transfer the juice to a covered shaker; add the vodka, Grand Marnier, and Southern Comfort. Shake until well blended. Pour the pineapple juice over ice in a highball glass. Garnish with a Pineapple, Orange, and Cherry Blossom (page 217), if desired.

Calories	425	Calcium	27 mg
Calories from fat	16	Iron	1 mg
Total fat	2 g	Vitamin C	60 mg
Carbohydrates	6 g	Folic acid	41 mcg
Protein	2 g	Magnesium	55 mg
Fiber	5 g	Potassium	443 mg

Fresh Pepper Bloody Mary

You can make this Bloody Mary hotter and spicier by adding the whole jalapeño pepper, but if you do, watch out—it's murder!

1 SERVING

4 plum tomatoes, halved

1 slice of lemon, peeled and cut ⅛-inch thick

½ (or more) jalapeño pepper, seeded

1 teaspoon minced cilantro leaves

½ teaspoon Worcestershire sauce

¼ teaspoon cumin

¼ teaspoon superfine sugar

1½ to 2 tablespoons vodka

Alternate adding the tomatoes, lemon, and jalapeño pepper to the juicer, and process until juiced. Place three ice cubes in an old-fashioned or tall glass, and add the juice, cilantro, Worcestershire sauce, cumin, and sugar. Mix well. Add the vodka and mix. Garnish with a celery stalk with leaves, if desired.

Calories	132	Calcium	23 mg
Calories from fat	10	Iron	2 mg
Total fat	1 g	Beta Carotene	1030 mcg
Carbohydrates	15 g	Vitamin C	78 mg
Protein	2 g	Folic acid	39 mcg
Fiber	3 g	Potassium	598 mg

Fuzzy Navel

The term fuzzy navel *refers to peach " fuzz" and a "navel" orange.*

1 SERVING

2 (or more) oranges, peeled and segmented

2 tablespoons peach schnapps

2 tablespoons vodka

Place the oranges in the juicer, and process until juiced; you want at least ¾ cup juice. Place three ice cubes in a tall glass; add the orange juice, schnapps, and vodka. Blend well. Garnish the rim of the glass with an Orange Wheel (page 211), if desired.

Calories	253	Calcium	105 mg
Calories from fat	3	Iron	0.27 mg
Total fat	0.31 g	Vitamin C	139 mg
Carbohydrates	31 g	Folic acid	79 mcg
Protein	2 g	Magnesium	26 mg
Fiber	6 g	Potassium	475 mg

Happily Ever Apple

Apples and clementines combined with apple liqueur are a marriage made in heaven. A definite cloud-nine experience.

1 SERVING

1 apple, cut into eighths

1 clementine, peeled and segmented

½ small lemon, peeled and halved

3 tablespoons Calvados, or other apple liqueur

Alternate adding the apple, clementine, and lemon to the juicer, and process until juiced. Place three ice cubes in a tall glass, and add the juice and apple liqueur. Mix well. Garnish the rim of the glass with a Lemon Wheel (page 211), if desired.

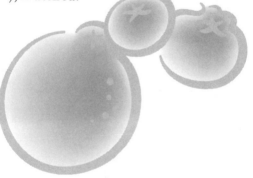

Calories	277	Calcium	29 mg
Calories from fat	8	Iron	0.53 mg
Total fat	0.87 g	Beta Carotene	497 mcg
Carbohydrates	52 g	Vitamin C	49 mg
Protein	1 g	Folic acid	24 mcg
Fiber	6 g	Potassium	337 mg

Hot Apple Brandy

After a day on the slopes, nothing warms you up faster than a stimulating cup of this apple drink.

1 SERVING

5 apples, cut into eighths

¼ cup apple brandy

1 (3-inch) cinnamon stick

4 cloves

Place the apples in the juicer, and process until juiced; you want at least 1¼ to 1½ cups juice. Transfer the apple juice to a small saucepan, and add the brandy, cinnamon, and cloves. Blend well. Heat over low heat for 30 minutes. Remove the cinnamon stick and cloves. Pour the Hot Apple Brandy into a coffee mug and enjoy.

Calories	536	Calcium	48 mg
Calories from fat	22	Iron	1 mg
Total fat	2 g	Beta Carotene	141 mcg
Carbohydrates	10 g	Vitamin C	39 mg
Protein	1 g	Magnesium	35 mg
Fiber	19 g	Potassium	295 mg

Laguna Peach Bellini

This drink says amore! *Serve it in the summer when peaches are at their ripest, and wait for the pinches.*

1 SERVING

2 peaches, pitted and quartered

½ cup champagne or sparkling wine

1 ½ tablespoons peach schnapps

Add the peaches to the juicer, and process until juiced. Pour the peach juice into a chilled champagne flute, and slowly add the champagne and schnapps. Lightly mix. Garnish with a Pineapple, Orange, and Cherry Blossom (page 217), if desired.

Calories	213	Calcium	10 mg
Calories from fat	2	Iron	0.22 mg
Total fat	0.18 g	Beta Carotene	521 mcg
Carbohydrates	25 g	Vitamin C	13 mg
Protein	2 g	Magnesium	14 mg
Fiber	4 g	Potassium	386 mg

Mai Tai

This delicious drink will take you to a tropical is-land on even the coldest of days.

2 SERVINGS

1 to 2 oranges, peeled and segmented

½ lemon, peeled and halved

1 cup cubed pineapple

6 tablespoons light rum

2 tablespoons orange curaçao

6 tablespoons dark rum

Add the oranges to the juicer and process until you have at least ¾ cup orange juice. Remove liquid from juicer and set aside. Next, add the lemon and process until you have at least ⅓ cup lemon juice. Remove juice from juicer and set aside. Lastly, add the pineapple to the juicer and process until you have at least ¾ cup pineapple juice. Pour the juices over crushed ice in a chilled hurricane glass, and add the light rum and orange curaçao. Mix well. Float the dark rum over the top of the drink, and garnish with a fresh orchid or a Pineapple, Orange, and Cherry Blossom (page 217), if desired.

Calories	304	Calcium	35 mg
Calories from fat	4	Iron	0.54 mg
Total fat	0.46 g	Vitamin C	54 mg
Carbohydrates	23 g	Folic acid	30 mcg
Protein	1 g	Magnesium	19 mg
Fiber	3 g	Potassium	228 mg

Mama Mimosa

Made with fresh orange juice, this drink is truly the mother of all mimosas.

1 SERVING

1 orange (or more), peeled and segmented

½ cup champagne or sparkling wine

Place the orange in the juicer, and process until juiced; you want at least ½ cup juice. Pour the orange juice into a champagne flute, and slowly add the champagne. Blend well. Garnish with a Pineapple, Orange, and Cherry Blossom (page 217), if desired.

Calories	141	Calcium	52 mg
Calories from fat	1	Iron	0.13 mg
Total fat	0.16 g	Vitamin C	70 mg
Carbohydrates	18 g	Folic acid	40 mcg
Protein	1 g	Magnesium	13 mg
Fiber	3 g	Potassium	237 mg

Orange Blossom

As fragrant and lovely as an orange blossom on a spring day, you will delight in the pleasure of this drink.

1 SERVING

1 orange (or more), peeled and segmented

2 tablespoons gin

Place the orange in the juicer, and process until juiced; you want at least ½ cup juice. Place three to four ice cubes in a highball or cocktail glass, and add the orange juice and gin. Blend well. Garnish the rim of the glass with an Orange Wheel (page 211), if desired.

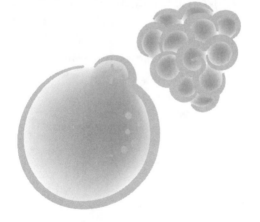

Calories	126	Calcium	52 mg
Calories from fat	1	Iron	0.14 mg
Total fat	0.16 g	Vitamin C	70 mg
Carbohydrates	15 g	Folic acid	40 mcg
Protein	1 g	Magnesium	13 mg
Fiber	3 g	Potassium	238 mg

Piña Colada

This popular tropical drink is fabulous when made with fresh pineapple juice. Who needs to go to an island when you can have it right in your own home?

1 SERVING

1 ½ cups cubed pineapple

½ cup crushed ice

¼ cup golden rum

3 tablespoons cream of coconut

Add 1 cup cubed pineapple to the juicer, and process until juiced. Transfer the pineapple juice to a blender; add the remaining ½ cup cubed pineapple, ice, rum, and cream of coconut. Mix until well blended. Pour the Piña Colada into a chilled hurricane glass, and garnish with a Pineapple, Orange, and Cherry Blossom (page 217) or a fresh orchid, if desired.

Calories	349	Calcium	17 mg
Calories from fat	97	Iron	1 mg
Total fat	11 g	Vitamin C	37 mg
Carbohydrates	33 g	Folic acid	33 mcg
Protein	2 g	Magnesium	42 mg
Fiber	4 g	Potassium	320 mg

Rum for Your Life

Not up to doing a 10K today? You'll feel just as invigorated after tasting this refreshing drink.

1 SERVING

¼ cup cubed pineapple

¼ cup cranberries

¼ lime, peeled

3 tablespoons light rum

½ tablespoon superfine sugar

Alternate adding the pineapple, cranberries, and lime to the juicer, and process until juiced. Transfer the juice to a covered shaker; add the rum and sugar, and shake until well blended. Pour the Rum for Your Life into a Tom Collins glass filled with ice. Garnish with a Lemon and Cranberry Twist (page 213), if desired.

Calories	156	Calcium	10 mg
Calories from fat	2	Iron	0.35 mg
Total fat	16 g	Beta Carotene	12 mcg
Carbohydrates	2 g	Vitamin C	14 mg
Protein	0.36 g	Magnesium	8 mg
Fiber	0.25 g	Potassium	79 mg

San Francisco

This drink is dedicated to my sons, David and Adam, happy San Franciscans. One taste of this fabulous drink, and you might leave your heart there, too.

1 SERVING

2 oranges, peeled and segmented

2 tablespoons vodka

2 tablespoons crème de banana

1 tablespoon grenadine

Place the oranges in the juicer, and process until juiced. Place three to four ice cubes in a highball glass, and add the vodka. First pour the orange juice over the vodka, then the crème de banana. Tilting the glass slightly, pour the grenadine on one side so it settles to the bottom of the glass. Garnish the rim of the glass with an Orange Wheel (page 211), if desired.

Calories	341	Calcium	106 mg
Calories from fat	4	Iron	0.32 mg
Total fat	0.41 g	Beta Carotene	102 mcg
Carbohydrates	59 g	Vitamin C	140 mg
Protein	2 g	Folic acid	80 mcg
Fiber	6 g	Potassium	485 mg

Screwdriver Squeeze

Put away the tool chest and tune up the juicer; with fresh orange juice this all-time favorite is better than ever.

1 SERVING

1 (or more) orange, peeled and segmented

3 tablespoons vodka

Place the orange in the juicer, and process until juiced; you want at least ½ cup juice. Place three to four ice cubes in a highball glass and add the orange juice and vodka. Mix well. Garnish the rim of the glass with an Orange Wheel (page 211), if desired.

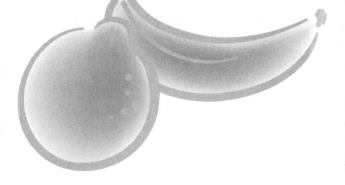

Calories	158	Calcium	52 mg
Calories from fat	1	Iron	0.14 mg
Total fat	0.16 g	Beta Carotene	51 mcg
Carbohydrates	15 g	Vitamin C	70 mg
Protein	1 g	Folic acid	40 mcg
Fiber	3 g	Potassium	238 mg

Shore Breeze

Angostura aromatic bitters are an extract from tropical herbs and spices. This recipe is an adaptation of one found on the label of the bottle. Using fresh juices elevates the cocktail to a new level of enticing flavor.

1 SERVING

1½ cups cubed pineapple

¼ cup cranberries

3 tablespoons light rum

2 dashes of angostura aromatic bitters

Alternate adding the pineapple and cranberries to the juicer, and process until juiced. Pour the rum into a hurricane glass, and add the juice and bitters. Lightly mix. Garnish by placing a wedge of pineapple and a maraschino cherry on the rim of the glass, if desired.

Calories	224	Calcium	17 mg
Calories from fat	9	Iron	0.96 mg
Total fat	1 g	Vitamin C	39 mg
Carbohydrates	32 g	Folic acid	25 mcg
Protein	1 g	Magnesium	34 mg
Fiber	4 g	Potassium	281 mg

Sunsplash

The Sunsplash cocktail was created in 1996 by a bartender at the Starlight Room in San Francisco. This is my freshly squeezed version of this Golden Gate grabber.

1 SERVING

1 orange, peeled and segmented

¼ cup cranberries

3 tablespoons vodka

1 tablespoon Cointreau

½ tablespoon superfine sugar

Alternate adding the orange and cranberries to the juicer, and process until juiced. Fill a covered shaker halfway up with ice, and add the juice, vodka, Cointreau, and sugar. Shake until well blended. Strain the Sunsplash into a chilled cocktail glass, and garnish with an Lemon and Cranberry Twist (page 213), if desired.

Calories	244	Calcium	54 mg
Calories from fat	2	Iron	0.20 mg
Total fat	0.25 g	Beta Carotene	58 mcg
Carbohydrates	1 g	Vitamin C	73 mg
Protein	4 g	Folic acid	40 mcg
Fiber	4 g	Potassium	257 mg

Tiger Jack

What a wonderful way to get your vitamin C!

1 SERVING

2 oranges, peeled and segmented

¼ cup Jack Daniels

2 tablespoons triple sec

½ tablespoon grenadine

Place the oranges in the juicer, and process until juiced. Fill a covered shaker halfway up with ice, and add the orange juice, Jack Daniels, and triple sec. Shake until well blended. Pour the grenadine into a chilled hurricane glass, and slowly add the juice mixture to the glass. Garnish with an Orange, Lemon, and Cherry Combo (page 215), if desired.

Calories	389	Calcium	106 mg
Calories from fat	4	Iron	0.31 mg
Total fat	0.40 g	Vitamin C	140 mg
Carbohydrates	51 g	Folic acid	79 mcg
Protein	2 g	Magnesium	27 mg
Fiber	6 g	Potassium	483 mg

Triple Sec Sunrise

This drink is reminiscent of the popular Tequila Sunrise. If you want a stronger drink, you may use additional triple sec.

1 SERVING

2 oranges, peeled and segmented

¼ cup triple sec

2 tablespoons grenadine

Place the oranges in the juicer, and process until juiced; you want at least ¾ cup juice. Pour the orange juice into a Tom Collins glass, and add the triple sec and grenadine. Blend well. Garnish with an Orange, Lemon, and Cherry Combo (page 215), if desired.

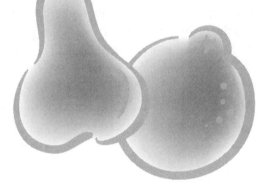

Calories	430	Calcium	108 mg
Calories from fat	5	Iron	0.37 mg
Total fat	0.50 g	Vitamin C	141 mg
Carbohydrates	85 g	Folic acid	80 mcg
Protein	3 g	Magnesium	28 mg
Fiber	6 g	Potassium	495 mg

Tropical-Squeezed Tisana

This is my fresh version of the popular Venezuelan drink.

2 SERVINGS

1 cup cubed pineapple

1 tangerine, peeled and segmented

1 apple, cut into eighths

1 peach, pitted and quartered

1½ teaspoons superfine sugar, or to taste

⅛ teaspoon angostura aromatic bitters

1 cup champagne or sparkling apple cider

Alternate adding the pineapple, tangerine, apple, and peach to the juicer, and process until juiced. Transfer the juice to a pitcher, and add the sugar, bitters, and champagne or cider. Mix lightly. Pour the juice into two chilled wineglasses and garnish the rim of each with a wedge of pineapple, if desired.

Calories	211	Calcium	19 mg
Calories from fat	6	Iron	0.51 mg
Total fat	0.71 g	Beta Carotene	385 mcg
Carbohydrates	36 g	Vitamin C	32 mg
Protein	1 g	Magnesium	12 mg
Fiber	5 g	Potassium	330 mg

Tropical Surprise

Whether it is a blustery, snowy day or a sultry, humid day, sit back, relax, and let this heavenly drink take you to paradise.

1 SERVING

2 oranges, peeled and segmented

1 cup cubed pineapple

¼ cup light rum

1 tablespoon dark rum

1 tablespoon coconut rum

2 teaspoons grenadine

Alternate adding the oranges and pineapple to the juicer, and process until juiced. There should be at least ¾ cup orange juice and ¾ cup pineapple juice. Transfer the juice to a small pitcher, and add the rums and grenadine. Lightly mix. Place four to five ice cubes in a chilled hurricane glass, and add the Tropical Surprise. Garnish with a fresh orchid or a Pineapple, Banana, and Cherry Charmer (page 216), if desired.

Calories	427	Calcium	117 mg
Calories from fat	9	Iron	0.96 mg
Total fat	0.99 g	Beta Carotene	120 mcg
Carbohydrates	60 g	Vitamin C	164 mg
Protein	3 g	Folic acid	96 mcg
Fiber	8 g	Potassium	655 mg

Yo Quiero Papaya-Banana Margarita

Even your Chihuahua will take notice when you serve this delicious margarita.

1 SERVING

Simple Lemon-Lime Syrup

3 tablespoons granulated sugar

3 tablespoons cold water

2 tablespoons fresh lemon juice

2 tablespoons fresh lime juice

Margarita

1 papaya, peeled, seeded, and cut into cubes

1 small ripe banana, peeled and cubed

3 tablespoons tequila

1 tablespoon triple sec

2 tablespoons simple lemon-lime syrup

Calories	405	Calcium	81 mg
Calories from fat	9	Iron	0.70 mg
Total fat	1 g	Vitamin C	203 mg
Carbohydrates	72 g	Folic acid	139 mcg
Protein	3 g	Magnesium	66 mg
Fiber	8 g	Potassium	1266 mg

To make the syrup
Combine the sugar and water in a small saucepan over medium heat for 6 to 8 minutes, or until the mixture comes to a boil. Remove the saucepan from heat; allow the mixture to cool to room temperature. When cool, add the lemon and lime juice and blend well. Transfer the syrup to a small covered container, and refrigerate for at least an hour or until well chilled.

To make the margarita
Add the papaya to the juicer, and process until juiced. Place the banana in a blender, and mix until pureed. Add the papaya juice to the blender; blend well. Add the tequila, triple sec, and Simple Lemon-Lime Syrup, and mix until well blended. Pour the margarita into a margarita glass, and garnish with a fresh orchid or a Lime Wheel (page 211), if desired.

CHAPTER 8

Garnishes with a Twist

As delicious and nutritious as a glass of fresh juice is, you might ask what more could you possibly do to improve it? The answer is that an ordinary-appearing glass of juice can become a work of art when served in an attractive glass and garnished with an extra twist of surprise. So, for those who want to go the extra mile when savoring a juice creation, I have included information on the different varieties of glassware that can be used to highlight a special juice, as well as several recipes that provide ideas for adding a garnish to your masterpiece. While some are quite elaborate, I have also included some very basic garnishes that may already be hidden in your refrigerator. Moreover, many of them can be interchanged or created from your favorite fruit or vegetable—just use your imagination and have fun.

If you don't have the time to prepare a garnish, you can simply visit your neighborhood party store and pick up some fun accessories such as decorative straws, cocktail umbrellas, bright-colored metallic sparklers, or colored stirrers. Who knows—once you experience the exhilaration of creative garnishing, you may never serve a plain beverage again!

Berries on a Skewer

A beautiful yet easy-to-prepare garnish that adds a rich color to most juices.

2 SKEWERS

½ cup raspberries (blueberries, cranberries, or blackberries)

2 (6-inch) wooden skewers

Alternate threading five to six berries of your choice on each skewer.

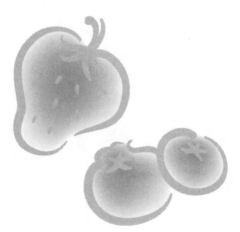

Calories	15	Calcium	7 mg
Calories from fat	2	Iron	0.18 mg
Total fat	0.17 g	Vitamin C	8 mg
Carbohydrates	4 g	Folic acid	8 mcg
Protein	0.28 g	Magnesium	6 mg
Fiber	2 g	Potassium	47 mg

Cucumber, Lemon, Lime, and Orange Wheels

If you have a garnishing set that includes a food decorator tool or canalling knife, follow the given instructions. If those tools are unavailable, then you will find the following technique, taught to me by my mother, is quite simple and requires only a fork.

8 WHEELS

1 cucumber (or lemon, lime, or orange)

Using a fork, start at one end of the cucumber (or other fruit), and move the fork down to the other end of the cucumber, slightly piercing the skin. Repeat this process around the entire cucumber. Remove the ends and cut the cucumber into ¼-inch thick slices. Make a slit by cutting through the peel and halfway into the flesh, and fit the slit over the rim of the glass.

Calories	0.53	Calcium	0.57 mg
Calories from fat	0.05	Iron	0.01 mg
Total fat	0.01 g	Beta Carotene	5 mcg
Carbohydrates	0.11 g	Folic acid	0.53 mcg
Protein	0.03 g	Magnesium	0.45 mg
Fiber	0.03 g	Potassium	6 mg

Fruit Skewers

These attractive garnishes can be made with any of your favorite fruits. It is nice to vary the color, shape, and texture, but there are no set rules.

2 SKEWERS

2 green grapes

2 pineapple cubes

2 kiwi slices

2 cantaloupe balls*

2 small strawberries

2 (6-inch) wooden skewers

Thread a grape, pineapple cube, kiwi slice, cantaloupe ball, and strawberry on a skewer. Repeat with the remaining skewer.

*Using a cantaloupe ball scoop, scoop out balls. (You may also simply cut the cantaloupe into cubes, if you like.) Thread three to four balls on each skewer.

Calories	31	Calcium	10 mg
Calories from fat	3	Iron	0.23 mg
Total fat	0.29 g	Beta Carotene	279 mcg
Carbohydrates	7 g	Vitamin C	29 mg
Protein	0.48 g	Magnesium	8 mg
Fiber	1 g	Potassium	137 mg

Lemon and Cranberry Twist

This versatile garnish can be made with an orange and blueberry, a lemon and blueberry, an orange and cranberry, a lime and cranberry, or any other combination that interests you.

2 TWISTS

2 lemon slices, each cut ¼-inch thick and halved

4 cranberries (or other berries)

2 (6-inch) wooden skewers

Thread a cranberry on a skewer, almost to the middle of the skewer. Place half a lemon slice on a plate so it looks like the letter *C*. Push the skewer through the skin near the cut end, and pass it *over* the flesh of the lemon to the other cut side, pushing it through the skin. Thread another cranberry on the skewer, and place it close enough to the lemon slice so the lemon slightly curls between the two cranberries. Repeat with the remaining half of the lemon slice, but place it on plate so it looks like a backward *C*. When the skewer is completed, the lemon halves should form an *S* shape.

Calories	3	Calcium	2 mg
Calories from fat	0.24	Iron	0.05 mg
Total fat	0.03 g	Beta Carotene	2 mcg
Carbohydrates	1 g	Vitamin C	4 mg
Protein	0.09 g	Folic acid	0.79 mcg
Fiber	0.32 g	Potassium	12 mg

Melon Balls on a Skewer

You will need a melon ball scoop to make the melon balls. It has two different-sized rounded spoons on each end and is available in gourmet food shops or the kitchen section of hardware stores. However, you can also cut out cubes of melon and the garnish will remain attractive.

2 SKEWERS

½ cantaloupe, honeydew, or watermelon, seeded

2 (6-inch) wooden skewers

Using a melon ball scoop, scoop out balls. Thread three to four balls on each skewer.

Calories	50	Calcium	20 mg
Calories from fat	0	Iron	0.36 mg
Total fat	0 g	Beta Carotene	2982 mcg
Carbohydrates	12 g	Vitamin C	48 mg
Protein	1 g	Potassium	280 mg
Fiber	1 g		

Orange, Lemon, and Cherry Combo

This garnish looks spectacular placed on the rim of the glass.

2 COMBOS

2 orange slices, each with skin and cut ¼-inch thick

2 lemon slices, each with skin and cut ¼-inch thick

2 maraschino cherries, with stem

4 mint leaves (optional)

Make a cut halfway up the orange and lemon slice. If using mint, place two mint leaves in each hole of the cherry where the pit was removed (if the pit remains, cut a small slit in the top). Cut a slit on the opposite side of the cherry. Using the slits cut in each fruit, place an orange slice, followed closely by a lemon, and then a cherry on the rim of each glass.

Calories	20	Calcium	8 mg
Calories from fat	0.37	Iron	0.06 mg
Total fat	0.04 g	Vitamin C	12 mg
Carbohydrates	6 g	Folic acid	6 mcg
Protein	0.23 g	Magnesium	2 mcg
Fiber	0.59 g	Potassium	39 mg

Pineapple, Banana, and Cherry Charmer

Like many garnishes, this one can be made with a variety of ingredients. The cherry can be replaced with a carrot slice; instead of parsley, try a sprig of carrot top; or use a small round of kiwi in place of the banana.

2 CHARMERS

2 pineapple wedges, with skin and cut ¼-inch thick

2 banana slices, with skin and cut ¼-inch thick

1 tablespoon fresh lemon juice

2 small sprigs parsley

2 stemless maraschino cherries

2 (6-inch) wooden skewers

Lightly brush the pineapple and banana with lemon juice to prevent them from turning brown. Thread a wedge of pineapple on a skewer, about a third of the way up the skewer. Thread the banana behind the pineapple, then wrap the stem of the parsley around the skewer, and, finally, add the cherry. Repeat with the remaining skewer.

Calories	21	Calcium	5 mg
Calories from fat	2	Iron	0.18 mg
Total fat	0.18 g	Beta Carotene	44 mcg
Carbohydrates	5 g	Vitamin C	9 mg
Protein	0.26 g	Folic acid	6 mcg
Fiber	0.56 g	Potassium	69 mg

Pineapple, Orange, and Cherry Blossom

The attractiveness of this impressive garnish belies its simplicity. It is also a delicious taste treat after the juice has been savored.

2 BLOSSOMS

2 stemless maraschino cherries

2 orange slices, each with skin and cut ¼-inch thick

2 wedges of pineapple, each with skin and cut ¼-inch thick

4 pineapple leaves, about 2½ inches long

2 (6-inch) wooden skewers

Thread a cherry on a skewer, almost to the middle. Add the slice of orange by pushing the skewer through the middle of the orange, followed by the pineapple wedge, and finally by the two pineapple leaves. Repeat with the remaining skewer.

Calories	28	Calcium	8 mg
Calories from fat	0.99	Iron	0.09 mg
Total fat	0.11 g	Beta Carotene	9 mcg
Carbohydrates	8 g	Vitamin C	12 mg
Protein	0.24 g	Folic acid	7 mcg
Fiber	0.65 g	Potassium	53 mg

Scallion Flower

Once you learn how to make these flowers, you not only will want to use them to garnish a drink but will also find that they can be used to dress up a salad or any meal when a dramatic touch is desired.

2 FLOWERS

2 scallions (or green onions)

Discard the root end of the scallion, and trim any brown edges on the green part. Insert the point of a needle (or a sharp paring knife) ½ inch from the root end, and carefully pull up through the scallion. Rotate the scallion slightly and repeat this process. Continue rotating the scallion and making cuts until it resembles a brush. Place the scallions in a bowl of ice water for 5 minutes, or until the scallion begins to curl. Drain well. When ready to use, insert a skewer into the root end of the scallion.

Calories	192	Calcium	4 mg
Calories from fat	0.10	Iron	0.09 mg
Total fat	0.01 g	Beta Carotene	14 mcg
Carbohydrates	0.44 g	Folic acid	4 mcg
Protein	0.11 g	Vitamin K	12 mcg
Fiber	0.16 g	Potassium	17 mg

SIMPLE GARNISHES

When your time is extremely short, preparing a special garnish for a juice or drink may not be possible. But with the variety of quick and easy greens and fruits available, as well as store-bought accessories, it is always possible to dress up a serving with almost no effort. I hope this list of simple garnishes will inspire you to keep a few of them on hand.

- Black or green olives on a toothpick
- Fruit chunks
- Maraschino cherries on a toothpick
- Mint leaves
- Orchids, preferably ones that have not been sprayed by a florist
- Parsley or watercress
- Pineapple chunks on a skewer
- Pineapple spears
- Pineapple wedges with leaves
- Straws that come in different twists, sizes, or colors
- Cocktail umbrellas
- Brightly colored metallic sparklers
- Colored stirrers

GLASSWARE

There is such an array of beautiful glasses available, it is hard to choose a favorite. They come in different sizes, shapes, and colors, and some are designed for special drinks. I will attempt to list the types of glasses most often suggested for particular drinks, but keep in mind that this list is meant to be informative and not an absolute requirement.

Champagne Flute

Champagne flutes are tall, stemmed glasses that hold between 6 and 8 ounces.

Large Goblets/Wine

Goblets can vary in size and shape, but all have curved sides and stems. They hold 8 to 14 ounces.

Brandy Balloon

These glasses are stemmed and somewhat shorter than wine goblets. The bowl is wider at the bottom and gradually narrows at the top. They hold between 6 and 24 ounces.

Collins

These stemless glasses are tall, straight-sided, and hold 10 to 14 ounces.

Highball

The highball glass is similar to a Collins except that it is smaller. It holds between 8 and 12 ounces.

Tumbler

Tumblers have sloping sides and hold about 4 to 8 ounces.

Hurricane

A hurricane is a stemmed glass that resembles a champagne flute, except the bowl is wider on the bottom, curves inward midway, and the rim flares out. It holds 15 ounces.

Cocktail/Martini

These stemmed glasses have a wide rim and a triangular or V-shaped bowl. They hold 4 to 6 ounces.

Old-Fashioned/Rocks

Old-fashioned glasses are squatty and stemless with a wide mouth; they hold between 6 and 10 ounces. Rocks are similar to old-fashioned glasses but sometimes have stems.

Double Cocktail

A double cocktail is similar to cocktail or martini glass but larger and more rounded. It holds 6 to 10 ounces.

Index

International Conversion Chart

These are not exact equivalents: they have been slightly rounded to make measuring easier.

Liquid Measurements

American	Imperial	Metric	Australian
2 tablespoons (1 oz.)	1 fl. oz.	30 ml	1 tablespoon
¼ cup (2 oz.)	2 fl. oz.	60 ml	2 tablespoons
⅓ cup (3 oz.)	3 fl. oz.	80 ml	¼ cup
½ cup (4 oz.)	4 fl. oz.	125 ml	⅓ cup
⅔ cup (5 oz.)	5 fl. oz.	165 ml	½ cup
¾ cup (6 oz.)	6 fl. oz.	185 ml	⅔ cup
1 cup (8 oz.)	8 fl. oz.	250 ml	¾ cup

Spoon Measurements

American	Metric
¼ teaspoon	1 ml
½ teaspoon	2 ml
1 teaspoon	5 ml
1 tablespoon	15 ml

Weights

US/UK	Metric
1 oz.	30 grams (g)
2 oz.	60 g
4 oz. (¼ lb)	125 g
5 oz. (⅓ lb)	155 g
6 oz.	185 g
7 oz.	220 g
8 oz. (½ lb)	250 g
10 oz.	315 g
12 oz. (¾ lb)	375 g
14 oz.	440 g
16 oz. (1 lb)	500 g
2 lbs	1 kg

Oven Temperatures

Farenheit	Centigrade	Gas
250	120	½
300	150	2
325	160	3
350	180	4
375	190	5
400	200	6
450	230	8